Stop drowning in your to-do list and start living
a more joyful creative life!

# OVERWHELMED WRITER RESCUE

## BOOST PRODUCTIVITY, IMPROVE TIME MANAGEMENT, AND REPLENISH THE CREATOR WITHIN

## COLLEEN M. STORY

MIDCHANNEL PRESS
www.midchannelpress.com

ALSO BY COLLEEN M. STORY

*Loreena's Gift*

*Rise of the Sidenah*

For more information, please see:

www.writingandwellness.com

www.colleenmstory.com

© 2017 by Colleen M. Story. All rights reserved.

No part of this book may be reproduced in any form or by any electronic or mechanical means including information storage and retrieval systems without written permission in writing from the publisher or author, except by a reviewer, who may quote brief passages in a review.

Although every precaution has been taken to verify the accuracy of the information contained herein, including Internet addresses, the author and publisher assume no responsibility for any errors or omissions. Further, the publisher does not have any control over and does not assume any responsibility for author or third-party websites or their content.

No liability is assumed for damages that may result from the use of information contained within. The author does not dispense medical advice or prescribe the use of any technique as a form of treatment for physical, emotional, or medical problems without the advice of a physician, either directly or indirectly. The intent of the author is only to offer information of a general nature to help you in your quest for physical, emotional, and creative well-being. In the event you use any of the information in this book for yourself, the author and the publisher assume no responsibility for your actions.

Books may be ordered through booksellers or by contacting the publisher at:

Midchannel Press
P.O. Box 52133
Idaho Falls, ID 83402
www.midchannelpress.com
Email: publisher@midchannelpress.com

To receive a free weekly e-mail newsletter delivering tips and updates about putting the power of *you* behind your best creative life, register directly at www.writingandwellness.com/newsletter.

Cover Design: Damonza.com
Interior Design: Damonza.com

ISBN 13: 978-0-9990991-0-0 (Paperback edition)
ISBN 13: 978-0-9990991-1-7 (eBook edition)

Library of Congress Control Number: 2017908998
1) Self-Help 2) Creativity 3) Time Management 4) Authorship

First Edition: September 2017, printed in the U.S.A.

*For any writer or creative artist struggling to keep his/her head above water, and to reconnect with the joy of the creative process.*

# CONTENTS

## Intro:
### Will Someone Please Give Me More Time to Write? | ix

Chapter 1: The Perfect Writing Life . . . . . . . . . . . . . . . . . . . . 1
Chapter 2: Time is in the Eye of the Beholder . . . . . . . . . . . . . . . 7
Chapter 3: Remember, You're Human . . . . . . . . . . . . . . . . . . 13
Chapter 4: Let It Go . . . . . . . . . . . . . . . . . . . . . . . . . . . . . 25

## Part II:
### Increase Productivity to Expand Your Writing Time | 41

Chapter 5: Prioritize . . . . . . . . . . . . . . . . . . . . . . . . . . . . . 47
Chapter 6: Arrest Your Time Thieves . . . . . . . . . . . . . . . . . . . 61
Chapter 7: Focus Faster . . . . . . . . . . . . . . . . . . . . . . . . . . . 71
Chapter 8: Know Your Time Personality . . . . . . . . . . . . . . . . . 85
Chapter 9: Say "No" . . . . . . . . . . . . . . . . . . . . . . . . . . . . 105
Chapter 10: Trick Yourself Into Getting Started . . . . . . . . . . . . 115
Chapter 11: Take a Break . . . . . . . . . . . . . . . . . . . . . . . . . . 125

## Part III:
### Outwit Your Brain's Productivity Saboteurs | 135

Chapter 12: Saboteur #1—Writer's Guilt . . . . . . . . . . . . . . . . 139
Chapter 13: Saboteur #2—Dis-ease . . . . . . . . . . . . . . . . . . . 153
Chapter 14: Saboteur #3—Self-Doubt . . . . . . . . . . . . . . . . . . 169
Chapter 15: Saboteur #4—Perfectionism . . . . . . . . . . . . . . . . 185
Chapter 16: Saboteur #5—Workaholism . . . . . . . . . . . . . . . . 195
Chapter 17: Saboteur #6—Destructive Goal-setting . . . . . . . . .201
Chapter 18: Saboteur #7—Belief . . . . . . . . . . . . . . . . . . . . . 213

## Part IV:
## Fail and Try Again | 221

Chapter 19: Use Your Motivation Style .................. 223
Chapter 20: Be Flexible and Persistent .................. 237
Chapter 21: Find Writer Solutions...................... 243
Chapter 22: Get Grit.................................. 257
Chapter 23: Answer Your Calling....................... 263

Note from the Author ................................ 265
References.......................................... 267
Acknowledgments ................................... 285
About the Author ................................... 287

# INTRO

## WILL SOMEONE PLEASE GIVE ME MORE TIME TO WRITE?

I SAT WITH ABOUT fifteen other writers. We'd all been to the same fiction workshop that day, and now we were gathered around a long, narrow table at a Mongolian restaurant for dinner. I was a full-time freelance writer, doing magazine articles, brochures, and research papers for clients during the day, and penning novels in my off hours. I'd been working hard on my fiction for years, but still hadn't received that coveted publishing contract I so desired. I was frustrated. It felt like my dream was within my reach, but that I was powerless to grasp it.

My problem, I was sure, was time. I just didn't have enough of it. I logged sixty or more freelance hours per week, performed on the French horn in several local groups, and gave private music lessons to students in the afternoons. All of these activities contributed to my income, and even though I was living frugally, there was no way to slow down and still keep everything afloat.

I knew that to reach my goal of becoming a published novelist, I needed more time to focus on the craft of fiction writing, but I just couldn't find it. I made sure to spend at least thirty minutes on my novels before work every day, but I always felt hurried, like I could just barely scratch the surface of my stories before I had to shift gears and write for somebody else.

If only I had more time, I believed, I could work more than a half-hour a day on my fiction, which would allow me to make faster progress. Then I could complete and submit more novels, and do more varied fiction work—maybe even a short story or poem. I could give myself more chances to make my dream come true.

Time was the key, I thought, but I had no idea how to find any more of it. I was starting to lose hope that I would ever become a published novelist, or that I would find a way out of the rat race I felt I was in.

I was drowning, frantically looking for a lifeline—for someone to tell me how to make more time in my life to write.

I had come to the dinner with high hopes. Surely among all these writers I could find someone like me, someone who had all the responsibility on her shoulders, and yet had found a way to make everything work. When the waiter came around the table with his pen and pad in hand, I placed my order, and then sat up straight, my ears straining on either side, hopeful that amidst the conversation I could glean the answer to all my problems.

It was a varied group that night: there was a couple that wrote and sold mystery books, the husband working part-time. Their books were earning money and they were very happy with their situation. A woman tech writer worked full-time for several government and technology companies in her area while writing fiction on the side, but publishing wasn't a driving ambition for her.

Another woman really wanted to find a publisher for her work, but her situation was far different from mine. She bragged about how her husband supported her financially and often took over household duties so she could spend her time writing. One older man was living on a healthy retirement pension and saw writing as only a fun pastime.

I heard all their stories. Not one of them was like mine.

I felt alone and isolated and mostly, in pain. It was my life's ambition to publish a novel, and it seemed like I was never going to make it. Worse, it wouldn't be because of a lack of desire, or discipline, or hard work, but because that monster time wouldn't stop for just one second to give me a chance to succeed. Holding my own book in my hands was my dream. I'd been raised to believe that if you worked hard enough, you could do anything, and for the most part, I'd found that to be true.

But not this time. Not with fiction writing.

I knew there had to be a solution. I fantasized about closing my business and getting by on my savings while writing to my heart's content. But the fear of what might come if the money ran out and I hadn't yet created a breakaway bestseller left me feeling more discouraged than ever.

I couldn't give up, though. Writing had a hold on me, its long, strong fingers encircled around my being. But I was stuck, lacking any real solution. So I went back to my usual routine: thirty minutes to an hour of fiction writing in the morning, hours of freelance work, music rehearsal and music lessons, and perhaps a blog post, some editing on the fiction I'd completed that morning, or website upkeep at night before I nodded off.

I plodded along like an old workhorse, slowed by the wound in my heart. I had very little hope that any of my work would come to fruition, and yet I couldn't stop.

Because you've picked up this book and are reading it, I have a feeling you may be at a similar point right now—one where you feel discouraged. Maybe you have a driving ambition to become a published writer, but so far, it hasn't happened, and like me, you blame time.

Or perhaps you've already published, and your days have turned crazy with marketing and blogging and keeping up with social media, leaving you little time to actually write anymore. Maybe you have a novel ready to go, but the idea of finding time to edit it, submit it to agents and editors, or self-publish and market it yourself seems so completely out of reach, it's laughable.

Maybe writing is all you've ever wanted to do, or maybe it's a new passion. Perhaps you, too, imagine holding your book in your hands, seeing your name on the cover, and signing your first copy. Or maybe you wish you could enjoy a less frantic life, one where you could maintain your author duties of marketing and blogging but still enjoy ample creative time.

You know you have it in you. But when you think about making it happen, you're at a loss.

That day at the workshop dinner, I was looking for a secret. I wanted someone to tell me how to change my life so I'd have more time for writing. I was hoping one of the other more experienced writers would share with me the key to it all.

When that didn't happen, I felt at a loss. And no wonder. Like many of us, I was looking for one solution, one grand truth that would suddenly make it all so much easier. It was only when I realized that no such solution exists that I finally started to find what really *does* work.

Turns out it's not about making some huge, drastic change so you suddenly have oceans of time to create. It's a romantic notion, this idea of walking away from the day job and spending every moment at the page—romantic and rarely realistic. Instead, true creative success is about all the little decisions you make each day that create the difference between wishing you could live your dream and actually living it.

Flash forward seven years later. After wondering for so long if I would ever see my fiction dreams come true, I finally have. I've had two novels traditionally published to date, and I'm working on a third. I'm happy to say I can finally call myself a novelist. I've held my books in my hands, and seen my name on the spines. I've read glowing reviews from my readers, had my work recognized in national literary contests, and enjoyed sold-out book signings.

I'm still a full-time freelance writer. I still manage all the finances by myself, and I still play French horn in the local symphony and pit orchestras.

What changed?

I'm excited to tell you, because I hope by sharing the secrets I've learned along the way, I can show you that you, too, *can* do this. You can wrestle time to the ground and make it work for you. You can become that person you've seen in your dreams, the one who proudly claims "writer" as part of his or her personae, or who finds time to write regardless of other marketing or publishing requirements. You can use these practical methods to bring sanity into your days, so you can stop feeling exhausted and get back to the joy of creation.

It's time to find time to write, not just today, but every day for the rest of your life.

## A Note About How to Use This Book

This book is titled *Overwhelmed Writer Rescue*, but it's easily applicable to any creative endeavor. The principles outlined here will work just as well for painters, musicians, and other creative artists, as it's all about making time in your life for your passion. I've stuck to the terms "writers" and "writing" throughout not to exclude other creative artists, but simply to make the book easier to read and follow.

You'll find throughout these pages sections entitled "Time Treasures." These are exercises designed to help you find more time in your life for writing (or other creative work), and are where you will discover the most practical tips. I encourage you to take an active approach to these sections, which will require that you set aside a separate notebook or computer file.

Finally, the book is organized into four parts:

1. **Part I** explains *why* you feel overwhelmed and like you never have enough time. Many factors contribute to that *always-busy-always-frantic* feeling. Some are a result of your unique point of view and some are by-products of our modern culture.

2. **Part II** provides straightforward, no-nonsense methods for increasing your productivity when you're writing, as well as when you're performing other important tasks in your life. You'll learn how to produce more creative work in less time,

and how to shrink the time needed for less important tasks and daily chores.

3. **Part III** helps you determine which facets of your personality are sabotaging your efforts to find more time in your schedule to write. Here you'll discover helpful tips for getting around those sneaky psychological land mines so you can get your writing done when you *do* have time for it.

4. **Part IV** shows you the final four skills you must learn to maintain productivity over a long-term creative career.

You may jump around the sections if you like, but traveling with me from front to back is the most effective way to clear the fog in front of you, discover and break through your own mental barriers, increase your overall productivity, and restore your creative work to its proper place in your life.

Ready for that lifeline? It's coming your way.

CHAPTER 1

# THE PERFECT WRITING LIFE

From where you're sitting right now, your dream of holding your own published book in your hands, or balancing writing with marketing without going crazy, may seem like an impossibility. After all, you just have too much going on in your life. So you fantasize about having the whole day to write, or better yet, the whole year. You imagine a life in which you're not pulled about so much, and you can just write to your heart's content. Ah, that would be bliss!

There's nothing wrong with wishing now and then, but for many writers, it can become extremely dangerous. That's because your idea of the perfect writing life could be stopping you from getting to the reality of what the perfect writing life actually *is*.

**Give Up the Idea of the Perfect Writing Life**

If you're like most creative people, you'd love to ditch your day job. You probably have a picture of the ideal writing situation in your head, and odds are it doesn't include eight hours working for someone else. If that picture isn't realistic, though, it can destroy your long-term plan, because it will sabotage the true path to success.

We all dream of what things *should* be like, how we should have hours every day to nurture our talent, or how we should be able to support ourselves with our creative work rather than with full-time employment at a job that doesn't utilize our gifts. Dreaming is fine… unless it stops you from progressing, and unfortunately, it often does.

Being faced with piles of bills and no rich uncle in sight gives most of us no choice but to maintain a day job. That relegates the creative work to those off hours, which aren't many. And if you're constantly imagining what it would be like to have loads of free time to create, those few hours you actually *do* have can seem pitifully inadequate by comparison. It's then that you fall into the trap of thinking, *Why bother? There's not enough time anyway.*

## Drop the "Perfect Situation" Fantasy

Here's the cold reality: Quitting a job to become a writer is an option only for the very few. Even successful fiction writers must do something else to supplement their income—most of them, anyway. According to a 2014 Digital Book World and *Writer's Digest* Author Survey, over half of traditionally published authors have yearly earnings of less than $1,000 a year. Only 1.3 percent of them earn more than $100,000 a year from their writing.

Yet all of those writers manage to continue to produce the creative work that matters to them, and so can you. It's time to disabuse yourself of the notion that you must quit your day job to succeed as a writer. You don't have to rid yourself of all the other tasks in your life to fulfill your creative potential. Instead, remind yourself:

"I don't have to quit my day job to make my dreams come true."

"I don't have to have a completely different life to enjoy my creative talent."

"I don't have to have the perfect situation to start working on the next step in my writing career, today!"

## "Working Harder" Isn't the Solution

Over the course of my life I've often thought that when things weren't going the way I wanted them to, I just needed to buckle down and work harder. The daughter of a strong Marine who served overseas and a woman raised by Irish Catholics, I was conditioned in the art of hard work. If I had dreams that weren't coming true, I was convinced I was slacking off.

It's true that hard work is needed. No one ever sat back in an easy chair and made it all happen. But it's also true that the opposite approach—having a bad case of "get-it-done-and-then-life-will-be-perfect-itis"—can lead to failure.

If you want your situation to change, you can't just leave everything as it is in your routine and expect you're going to get your writing done. It hasn't worked so far. Why would it work now? And if you think that doing your darnedest to get everything else done *faster* will magically produce the perfect writing life, well, good luck with that.

I can tell you firsthand that working harder rarely works, and if it does, it doesn't last long. You may be able to step up your efforts for a few weeks and squeeze more writing time in, but pretty soon you'll be right back where you started—burned out, discouraged, and afraid your dreams are receding from view.

Here's the real truth:

> There will never be a time when everything in your life is done, set, and perfectly in order, and you can just sit back, relax, and write.

You may believe you can furiously follow your to-do list until it's done and then sink into that couch and write your heart out. Even if you succeed for a day or two, you'll likely be exhausted by the time you finish your other chores, and you probably won't be happy with what you've created. This is just not a permanent fix.

There will always be tasks to do, broken items to be repaired, places to go, appointments to keep, people to help, socks to wash, and unexpected events that zoom in and take up time. That's life. I must say it again, because deep in our subconscious minds, many of us still believe this is true.

> There will never be a time when everything in your life is done, set, and perfectly in order, and you can just sit back, relax, and write.

That means you must make the life you have *now* work for you, creatively. Stop dreaming of the perfect writing life and start, instead, working on how you're going to change the life you have.

The change you must make is in how you manage your time. Yes, time management skills, especially in today's fast-paced world, are critically important for creative people. It's a shame most of us were taught so little about it when we were growing up, or at any time since, because the more technology penetrates our lives, the more we need these skills to keep our heads above water, never mind tending to our creative callings.

The good news is that these skills are easy to learn, and they can be applied again and again, even as your life evolves, so you can always make room for writing. Initially, it will take some effort to incorporate your new skills into your daily life, but after the first few weeks, they'll start to become habits. By the time you finish this book, you'll not only have found a way to fit more writing time into your schedule, but you'll also feel less hurried, rushed, stressed, and exhausted.

Best of all, you'll feel more like "you." By spending quality time on your creative pursuits, you'll restore yourself to yourself, and that's the fastest way to inner peace and fulfillment.

---

Time Treasure

## Embrace Your Life Just As It Is

The first step you need to take on this journey is to embrace your life just as it is. Get clear with yourself that at least for now, the "perfect" writing life, whatever that may be for you, is not likely to drop into your lap anytime soon. Instead, it's time to accept the life you do have, and start figuring out how you can fit more creative time into it.

Promise yourself that at least for the duration of time it takes to read this book, you will stop:

- Complaining that your life isn't more "writer-friendly."

- Wishing you could come into a large inheritance so you could quit your day job.

- Longing for a sugar daddy or sugar mama to come along and happily support your writing habit.

- Wishing that your life would magically change, because you assume you'll never reach your dreams the way it is now.

> Your life can be different, and I'm going to show you how to make it so, but for now it's important that we start from ground zero. No matter what your life is like, it's okay. We can work with it. Where you are is just fine.

CHAPTER 2

# TIME IS IN THE EYE OF THE BEHOLDER

Despite the fact that we all have twenty-four hours in each day, that time is frequently devoured by tasks and activities that seem less important than writing. As a result, we often end up feeling like we never have enough time to write. Why does this happen, when writing is so important to us?

Most of us feel we have no choice in the matter: a lot of that time goes into work and the mundane business of life. The *real* reason we may feel so completely robbed of time, though, is not time itself, but our perception of it. You may remember the old saying, "Beauty is in the eye of the beholder." The same could be said about time—it's all in how you perceive it.

Think about a recent event you really enjoyed. Maybe you were spending time with loved ones, doing something you like such as skiing or hiking, or working on a piece of writing that was flowing with ease.

Now think about a recent event you did *not* enjoy. Maybe you went to the dentist, renewed your license at the DMV, or waited in line at the grocery store. How did your perception of time change in each of these instances? It probably flew by when you were enjoying yourself, but crawled when you weren't.

Time is all about perception, and how much you think you have for activities such as writing often has more to do with how you feel than about what actually shows on the face of your watch. Becoming more aware of this phenomenon can help you start to regain control of your schedule, no matter how crazy it may seem.

## Emotions Affect How We Perceive Time

Scientists have discovered that emotions affect the perception of time. In a 2011 study, researchers showed each participant one of three different types of movies:

1. a scary one,
2. a sad one, and
3. a neutral one.

Afterward, they asked everyone to complete a separate task measuring perception of time. After the sad and neutral films, participants were able to guess how much time had passed in the subsequent task with reasonable accuracy. After the scary film, though, they guessed wrong; they thought that the subsequent task lasted longer than it really did. Researchers believed that a state of heightened arousal sped up the participants' internal clocks.

When you're happy and energetic, even unpleasant tasks seem manageable, as they seem to go by more quickly. When you're feeling stressed, however, formerly simple tasks like doing the dishes can stretch on forever. Once you realize this, and you think about the many emotions you experience every day, it's easy to see how much your own psychological state affects your perception of time. You may feel like you're constantly running out, but that may have more to do with how much stress you're under than how many hours you actually have in the day.

## Time Passes Quickly or Slowly Depending on Attention Level

The level of attention applied to a task can also make a big difference in how long it seems to take. Studies show that paying *more* attention to what we're doing slows perception down. If you're knee-deep in writing a story, for example, you may look up and be surprised at how much time has gone by. This can make it seem like you never have enough time to write, because the time you do have goes by so quickly.

In a 1985 study, researchers found that the more difficult the task, the worse students were at accurately judging how much time had passed. They found similar results in 2010, and theorized that because more of the brain was involved in the task, less was available to accurately judge the passing of time.

There are few tasks that require more brainpower or attention than writing, so it's no wonder that time can fly by when we're doing it. Performing more mundane tasks, on the other hand, causes the opposite misjudgment. If you're filing papers, for example, or adding up figures, you may find yourself watching the clock. *Gee, it's only three in the afternoon? I thought it was near quitting time.*

## Technology Creates the Illusion that Time is Whizzing By

Technology has become another major factor in how we perceive time. We spend our days on our computers, smartphones, and tablets and communicating through social media. This increasing reliance on gadgets makes it feel like time is flying by faster than it used to, according to psychology researcher Dr. Aoife McLoughlin of James Cook University in Australia.

In one of her studies, for example, those who were frequently online tended to overestimate how much time had passed, and were also more likely to feel like time was running out, compared to those who rarely used technology.

This sense of time speeding up not only makes us feel like the day is getting away from us, but can also give us the feeling of being pressed for time, which results in that stressed-out scenario we all hate. If you're feeling this way, it could be that technology is at least partially to blame.

### The Power of Conditioning

How you actually spend your time each day will also affect your perception of how much you have. Here's an example that may be familiar, especially if your mother insisted you fold every freshly laundered piece of clothing a certain way. Chances are, you still fold to her standards, which means you continue to spend extra time folding laundry decades later, without even realizing it. (Those socks must be tucked inside one another, right side out!) That's the power of conditioning.

All of us have been conditioned in one way or another to spend time on things that perhaps aren't all that important, but we haven't stopped to think about it. Unfortunately, that conditioning makes us less efficient than we could be, and also means we end up spending too much time on things that don't really matter—and not enough on those that do, like writing.

**Stop Feeling Like a Victim**

We all have demands on our time, but it's important not to fall into the trap of believing you're a victim to the clock. That leaves you feeling powerless and unable to change things. The truth is that once you know how to pull away and avoid being ruled by assumed obligations and responsibilities, you'll stop feeling there is no way out. There is a way, and I'm going to show you how to find it.

For now it's enough to know that emotions, attention level, technology, and conditioning can all affect how you perceive time, and if you're not careful, may leave you feeling like there's no way you can fit in one more thing—even your writing.

Overcoming these feelings will help you to get closer to living the type of life you want to live, where you have time each day to relax and write. You must become independent of outside (and even inside!) forces that threaten to steal your time away, or convince you that you don't have any. You are the master of your universe; when you realize this, you can start setting up your day more to your liking.

CHAPTER 3

# REMEMBER, YOU'RE HUMAN

Our world is different today than it was twenty, or even ten, years ago.

It used to be that everyone did one thing at a time. Workers went to the office or the plant or the restaurant and worked, and stay-at-home moms focused on raising kids and keeping up with the household duties. When work was over, employees went home and relaxed. When it was time to eat, families gathered around the table. When dinner was over, they cleaned up and then enjoyed some leisure time. When they wanted to socialize, they went to each other's houses or to a central meeting place, enjoyed the company of others, and then went home. For entertainment, they went to movies or concerts or watched television shows and were present in the moment until the program was over. When the day was done, they turned the lights off and went to bed.

Enter the smartphone and everything changed. Now, people do all of this *at the same time*. They socialize on Facebook and Twitter in the middle of the workday, and often steal time to entertain themselves with YouTube videos or various websites. When they go home, they don't necessarily stop working. They answer emails and take calls from coworkers. Families rarely sit down to eat anymore—they eat on the run. If they actually do sit down, members have their phones with them, checking on friends, looking at amusing things, or responding to texts and emails. People do housework while they're on the phone or listening to a podcast. When they go out to a concert, half their attention is on the show, and half on sharing the moment with friends and Facebook connections.

Even when on vacation, people take it all with them—the work, the friends, the family, and the entertainment. They try to get real time away, but feel pulled back when a work colleague emails, or when the neighbor has a question about the pet sitter. Many people can't even go to sleep without having their smartphones nearby.

It's like carrying everything around with us in a giant backpack twenty-four hours a day. Problem is, we're not built to operate this way.

## Multitasking Reduces Productivity

We've come to know this combining of activities as "multitasking," the art of doing two or more things at the same time. Many of us think it works, but scientists say it's actually quite impossible. We don't really do more than one thing at a time. Instead, the brain switches rapidly from one task to the other, going back and forth like Lucille Ball trying to quality check one chocolate and then the next on the assembly line. And just like she fights a losing battle, so does everyone else.

Every time you switch from one task to the other, there is a cognitive cost. You have only so much energy in the bank, and every time you cook dinner and check up on Facebook posts at the same time, you use some of it up.

Researchers out of Stanford University discovered via a series of tests with a hundred participants that those who could focus on one thing at a time significantly outperformed those who kept switching back and forth, and who were distracted by other information. In fact, the ones who said they were regular multitaskers performed horribly.

You may think you're "multitasking" when you switch from working on a project to answering a text or email, but you're actually distracting yourself from the original task. This reduces your productivity, some studies say by as much as forty percent. Scientists have gone so far as to conclude that multitasking reduces intelligence, causing a greater temporary decrease in IQ than smoking marijuana or losing a night's sleep.

Multitasking steals your energy, as well. Every time you shift your attention, you work the brain, which requires fuel. Soon you're likely to feel tired and disoriented, and you may crave carbohydrates. Not good for the waistline. Repeated task switching has also been connected to anxiety, which raises levels of the stress hormone cortisol. All these effects create a very tiring, aggravating day, and take you far from the goals you want to reach.

Staying on task, on the other hand, uses less energy, reduces the brain's need for fuel, helps you maintain a sense of calm, and propels you to finish what you're doing on time so you can get your writing done, too.

## People Are Not Machines

Technology has put the world in our hands, which in many ways is an amazing thing. But it's also presented us with some new challenges. As computers become more intertwined with our daily lives, we are actually trying to become more like them.

According to author Melissa Gregg, as computers became more

commonplace at work, employees began to feel like they had to keep pace with them, i.e., get more done in less time and multi-task frequently. That desire led to longer work hours: "The consumer appetite for productivity techniques reflects an environment in which work has spilled over from the office to the train, airplane, hotel room, even bed," said Gregg in her piece "The Productivity Obsession," published in *The Atlantic*.

Rather than complain about the situation, however, many employees wear their busyness as a badge of honor. There's the feeling that being in constant demand equals importance. It doesn't help when the employees who are available for work purposes 24/7—either in the office or on the phone—are the ones singled out for rewards.

If you're like most writers, you are an entrepreneur at heart, trying to start your own business on the side. That translates into snatching every spare minute to work on something that will push that business forward. You probably realize the importance of having a platform, which means whenever you're not working the day job, you need to be building a website, blogging, posting, sending out newsletters, and more. Unfortunately, this constant "doing" takes its toll on creativity and personal well-being.

## Information Overload Increases Stress

I'm probably not telling you anything you don't already know about the perils of being *on* twenty-four hours a day. Stress, fatigue, headaches, muscle aches, insomnia, and irritability are just some of the side effects. To maintain your health and creativity and to stay on the path to your writing dreams, you need to incorporate some down time into your daily routine.

We're all victims, to some extent, of the "always-on" culture. It's easy to get burned out when we travel with technology all the time and work at all hours, even taking phones with us to bed. Parents are often said to work "triple shifts," because they return to work via their computers, tablets, and phones after putting the kids down for the night.

It's not just work, either. We are exposed to more data and information today than we have ever been in the entire history of the human race. By some estimates, we spend more hours consuming media than we do sleeping! A Pew Research Center report stated: "There is more information flowing into people's lives now than ever—much of it distressing and challenging. There are more possibilities for interruptions and distractions....These technologies are said to take over people's lives, creating time and social pressures that put people at risk for the negative physical and psychological health effects that can result from stress."

It can be exhausting trying to filter through all the information available to us today, and to decide what to pay attention to and what to ignore. Just that task alone adds to the daily to-do list.

Plus, people just plain have to do more these days. There are fewer travel agents to book trips and vacations, because there are websites that allow people to do it themselves. Home Depot and similar stores encourage do-it-yourself home projects (forget the contractor), and online shopping (without the help of a sales associate) is all the rage. The U.S. Postal Service is even encouraging customers to weigh packages and print postage at home to cut down on the need for postal workers. (It saves a trip to the post office, they say, but on that trip you might have gotten some creative daydreaming done in the car, at least!)

In fact, as you start to look closely at how we're living today, you can see more clearly why you may feel like you're always behind.

## Put Down the Phone

On some level, you know that overusing your smartphone is an addictive habit, and like any habit, it's hard to break. You're not alone. A 2014 study from Baylor University found that about sixty percent of students admitted they could be addicted to their phones, and experienced restlessness and agitation when the gadgets were out of sight. Women college students spent an average of ten hours a day on their cell phones, and men about eight hours a day.

This addiction, as I've learned from experience, seems to get worse as our phones become capable of performing more tasks. We can stay in touch with loved ones and work colleagues, do research, maintain a website, monitor workouts, check the weather forecast, record our thoughts, keep notes, take photos, and the list goes on. It's a consistent spiral of activity that doesn't allow the brain to slow down and just space out.

It's especially horrible for we creative writers who need down time—boredom even—to nurture our ideas. We must have that mental space. Without it, ideas run stale and creative energy disappears.

## Boredom Has its Benefits

Think back to the last time you were bored. I'm betting you probably can't remember, unless it was in a doctor's waiting room or in the middle of a traffic jam. We tend to pack our schedules from dawn to dusk and beyond (and still don't accomplish all we set out to do), and when we do get that spare moment, we fill it by consuming information and entertainment on our gadgets, prohibiting even the slightest hint of boredom.

This habit robs us of the gifts that being bored can give us. Imagine two scenarios: In the first, you rush home after a stressful day and plop down for thirty minutes to write. In the second, you do the same, except you spend fifteen minutes reading a phone book before you start to write. Decide which of those two scenarios you think would result in more creative writing, and then consider this: Researchers discovered in 2014 that doing something boring (like reading a phone book) before doing something creative resulted in *more* creative work. They theorized that during the boring activity, participants engaged in daydreaming, which encouraged creativity in the next task.

Now imagine watching a video clip designed to elicit one of four emotions:

- Elated
- Relaxed
- Bored
- Distressed

You can probably already guess which video resulted in higher levels of creativity. Those who were "primed" with the boring video performed more creatively than any of the other three groups. The point is that boredom stimulates creativity—"busyness" does not.

Writing in the journal *Frontiers in Psychology*, researcher Andreas Elpidorou of the University of Louisville stated: "…boredom motivates the pursuit of a new goal when the current goal ceases to be satisfactory, attractive, or meaningful….Boredom is both a warning that we are not doing what we want to be doing and a 'push' that motivates us to switch goals and projects."

It used to be that in response to sitting around the house being bored, kids would find creative ways to fill up their days. Now they have so many options for entertainment—on their computers, tablets, and phones—that inventing ways to use a cardboard box is no longer a necessary task. Adults are in the same boat. Instead of turning to writing or some other creative pursuit during a boring afternoon, we tend to pull up a game, video, movie, or some other form of electronic entertainment instead.

## How Much Downtime Do You Get Each Week?
For a quick self-assessment, answer the following questions:

1. About how much time each week do you spend being bored?
    a. less than an hour
    b. 1-2 hours
    c. 3 hours
    d. 4 hours or more
2. How much downtime do you typically get on the weekend (not counting sleeping time)?
    a. 8 hours or more
    b. 5-7 hours
    c. 2-4 hours
    d. 2 hours or less
3. How much downtime do you get on a typical weekday (not counting sleeping time)?
    a. 3 hours or more
    b. 2-3 hours

c. about an hour

d. less than an hour

4. How much time do you currently have per week to spend doing as you like?

   a. 8-10 hours or more

   b. 6-8 hours

   c. 4-6 hours

   d. less than 4 hours

Add up your A, B, C, and D answers. The more As you have, the better for your creativity. More Bs and Cs means you're doing "okay," but could do better. The more Ds you have, the more likely you are to feel stressed, worn out, and anything but creative! The solution is to address these issues so you can carve more downtime out of your week…and eventually more writing time.

## Time to Choose

If you're not careful about the choices you make, the following things can lead to feeling that you never have enough time:

- information overload
- multi-tasking
- pressure to *do more*
- gadgets that make it possible to take work wherever you go
- the temptation to stay in touch with friends, family, acquaintances, and mere online connections 24/7
- over-availability of media entertainment

- lack of downtime (and boredom)

The good news is that they can *all* be brought under your control, even if it doesn't feel like it right now. You can decide how you respond to all these circumstances and others in your life that make you feel pressed for time, once you learn new skills in time management: things like how to set specific times for dealing with each individual issue, for example, and learning how to set priorities for what's most important to you.

Before you can move up to that step, though, you have to change your mindset about technology. This can be difficult, but when you really think about it, technology is a mixed blessing. Ask most people and they will say they love how technology has opened up new worlds for them, but they'll also bemoan how it hogs their time. Most are really attached to their cell phones, even if they're not actually addicted. They love having the Internet so easily available, being able to quickly get in touch with loved ones, and having the luxury of watching videos and playing electronic games whenever the mood strikes.

But these distractions rob time from your creative calling. No matter how shiny all those fun things are, something else is whispering in your ear, and it's time to stop ignoring it. It's time to get serious—or *more* serious—about your creative aspirations.

Time Treasure

## Practice Boredom

Choose one day this week when you can block out one hour to do *nothing*. You can go for a walk or choose a special location like a park or the library, and take with you *only* a blank notebook and a pen. Nothing else. No books, no tablet, no cell phone.

Give yourself that hour to be bored. Your only solace is your notebook, in which you can doodle, jot down ideas that come to you, compose poetry or prose, or whatever occurs to you, but do your best not to give yourself an assignment beforehand. This is about letting the power of boredom spark something new inside you.

After an hour has passed, abandon your notebook for at least a day before you review your ideas/drawings/poetry. If you are excited about what you see, or feel that sense of new creativity, schedule an hour for the following week. Eventually, you can make this a regular part of your creative practice.

CHAPTER 4

# LET IT GO

IMAGINE IT'S A hot summer day, and you've just walked into an ice cream parlor. There you are with all those luscious choices in front of you. You're in ice cream heaven! But it's so difficult to choose.

Finally, you make a decision, but even as the server scoops out that creamy goodness, your eyes drift to the other flavor you *didn't* select. You wonder if you should have picked that one instead. Soon you hold the cone in your hand and you take that first bite. Delicious! The second bite is just as satisfying. But then you start to experience flavor fatigue. You're still enjoying the cone, but part of you feels like you missed out. You vow to try the other flavor next time.

This ice cream metaphor is typical of our lives today. Presented with umpteen choices of what to do with our time (write a story, stream a movie, try a new video game, talk with friends online, watch television, etc.), we should be in hog heaven. Instead, too many choices often make us *unhappy,* and cause us to make poor decisions when it comes to time management.

**Limited Options Are Best**

Although you may like the idea of a lot of choices, when it comes to actually being faced with them, I'm sure you'll agree it can be overwhelming. Just think back to the last time you tried to choose a new toothbrush. They have rows and rows of them now, and it's like you need a Ph.D. in dental care to figure out which one is best for your teeth.

Indeed, most of us feel not only baffled when presented with endless choices, but stressed out, too. We may think that more is better, but it's just not true.

Researchers proved it in the famous "jam" study. They set up a tasting booth that displayed either an extensive (twenty-four) or limited (six) number of jars of jam. They then sat back and watched as the shoppers came by. In the end, more customers stopped to look at the extensive tasting booth (sixty percent) than the limited tasting booth (forty percent), but when it came to actually *buying* the jam, more customers purchased from the limited booth (thirty percent) than the extensive booth (three percent).

The study results seem counter-intuitive; we imagine we'd prefer having more choices, not fewer. But the truth is that when faced with too many options, the brain shuts down. In one study, volunteers were presented with a financial-related scenario and asked to choose the one option out of sixteen that would provide the best payoff. If they made the right choice, they were paid twenty-five dollars.

Researchers then asked participants to use each of the three decision-making approaches below, for three tries at the test:

1. **Simultaneous choice**: Consider all sixteen options, and then choose one.

2. **Sequential elimination**: Choose one of four options, and watch the other three disappear, to be replaced by new options. Then choose one again. Repeat until you have one final choice.

3. **Sequential tournament**: Choose one of four options repeatedly, until you're faced with your final four, and from there, make your final selection.

Results showed that when participants used the sequential tournament method in making their selections (choosing one out of four repeatedly), they made the best decisions. When they used the simultaneous choice (considering all sixteen options at once), they made the worst decisions.

Would you be surprised to learn that the participants preferred the simultaneous choice? Pick one and done. They were unaware, though, that this would result in their worst decisions.

Study author Tibor Besedeš, associate professor of economics at the Georgia Institute of Technology, noted that when humans have fewer items from which to choose, they make better decisions.

This is why you may end up being unproductive when you have a seemingly unlimited number of options. Imagine, for instance, that you receive the unexpected gift of a free evening. Since it comes as a surprise, you're overwhelmed with alternatives: work on your writing, watch television, clean up the messy house, catch up on emails, post something interesting on Facebook, or take a nap. If you don't deliberately choose an activity to focus on, you're more likely to waste that time.

Indeed, being faced with too many choices creates inaction. Researchers found this to be true when they offered students extra credit for writing a two-page essay. Students were given either six or thirty potential essay topics. Though the majority of the class agreed to do the extra-credit assignment, those presented with fewer essay topics were more likely to actually complete and turn in the assignment than those presented with more essay topics (seventy-four percent compared to sixty percent).

And here's something to remember: Those in the limited-choice group wrote essays that were *of higher quality*, and scored higher than those in the extensive-choice group.

## Too Many Decisions Can Weaken Your Willpower

Too many choices simply stresses us out. Think of your life. Every day, from dusk until dawn, you're bombarded with choices of what to do with your time, money, and thoughts. If you choose to watch the news, your thoughts will be directed toward the featured headlines. If you choose to browse the Internet, your time is frittered away consuming information and advertisements. If you choose to browse your Facebook or Twitter feeds you could be so overwhelmed with things to read that you take time away from eating a healthy breakfast or perhaps exercising.

So it goes all day long. By the time the day is done, you're exhausted and don't want to make one more decision.

"Honey, what do you want for dinner?"

"I don't care! Whatever. You decide."

That means if you don't already have a set schedule in mind for how you're going to spend your days (including when you're going to write), you can quickly become sidetracked. It's too easy to get overwhelmed and end up making poor decisions that don't support your long-term goals.

To make sure that you have time to write, schedule that time, and then limit your options. That's why I recommend you turn off the television, silence the phone, get off the Internet, close the door, and refrain from doing anything else that will take your focus away from the task at hand. In short, don't give yourself the choice to do anything but create.

## Write When Your Brain is Alert

Not only does having too many choices stress you out, it also tires the brain. This is why it can feel so good to let someone else take charge.

Making a decision requires tapping into the brain's "executive function," which uses energy *no matter how simple the decision*. Even if you're just deciding whether or not to eat a cookie, you're using this executive function, which scientists equate to a muscle. And like any muscle, the more you use it over the course of the day, the more fatigued it gets, and the worse it performs. If you try to write at the end of the day, you may not be very productive because your brain will be tired and more vulnerable to distractions.

We know that after running four miles or spending all day baby-sitting a toddler, we're going to feel worn out. What we may not realize is that *mental* activities, particularly making multiple decisions, can be just as tiring as physical ones, and can make it more difficult to stick with a prior commitment, even if that commitment is to something important like writing.

There's no question that creativity requires a lively brain. When you deplete your brainpower during the day, your willpower will suffer when you face the blank page at night. If you've experienced this, don't be too hard on yourself. You're only human. You may have caved into fatigue, but you probably made a lot of decisions that day, and were simply tired.

The solution is to become more aware of how your brain works. If writing at the end of the day means dealing with decision-making fatigue, maybe the time to write is earlier, when your decision-making muscle is still strong. Another option is to cut back on the number of decisions you make so you're still fresh with enough self-discipline to write instead of watching TV. If you have a supportive partner, you can enlist his or her help in making sure you stick to your commitments.

> **Time Treasure**
>
> ## Limit Your Decisions
>
> Every day, you make a constant stream of decisions, from the simple to the important in your business and personal life. Look over your daily schedule and see where you're requiring yourself to make decisions that could be eliminated. There's a reason Apple founder Steve Jobs wore the same outfit to work every day (black turtleneck and jeans): he didn't want to waste his mental energy deciding what to wear.
>
> You don't have to adopt a boring wardrobe, but you can take similar actions to ease up on decision fatigue. Lay out your clothes the night before, for example. Decide on your meals a week ahead of time, use your Saturday morning to plan out the week's events on the calendar (and then resist changing them), and allow your partner to make some decisions such as where you're going to eat on date night.
>
> Then apply this same principle to your writing time. Decide beforehand where you will sit when it's time to write, where you will put your cell phone (so it doesn't distract you), how long you will write, how you will keep the Internet and

> email from interrupting you, and what project you will work on. Ask family members not to bother you between the hours you have set aside. Make sure your writing materials are easily accessible, and that your television is not. Do everything you can to make it a simple thing to just sit down and write.
>
> Think of the runner who leaves her sneakers by the bed each night to be sure she runs first thing the following morning, or the commuter who carpools so there's no debate on when she will leave work (she has to be ready at the right time to catch her ride). Approach your writing time with that mindset.
>
> Limit decisions. Make it easy to follow through.

## Time Requires Sacrifice

It's true that making fewer decisions, limiting your access to technology when you need to, and creating more downtime in your life will all help open up more space in your day for writing, but there's no way around it: even with these changes, you're going to have to sacrifice something to find time for your creative work.

The truth is that resistance to sacrifice is one of the main reasons it's so difficult to manage time. It's too hard to give anything up.

See how many of the following excuses you've used:

- I could wake up an hour earlier in the morning, but… (I love sleeping in, etc.)
- I could work on my lunch hour, but…
- I could try writing on the train on the way home, but…
- I could maybe fit in an hour on the weekend, but…

...and I'm sure there are many more you could add.

No matter what your situation—how busy and crazy your life is—if you want to find time to do your creative work, you must sacrifice something else.

No one likes hearing this cold, hard fact. We'd rather find an app or computer gizmo to do stuff faster. These apps and tools do exist, but they can't magically create the time needed to write. Remember that it takes time to learn how to work any new app or program, and even more time to figure out how to fit it into your daily life. Once you do, it often turns out that it actually requires *more* of your time rather than less.

You have twenty-four hours in the day and nothing is going to change that. If an app helps free up ten or fifteen minutes, great, but that's all it's going to accomplish. Hardly enough time to get a significant amount of writing done.

## Choose What to Let Go

I've sacrificed many things to make time for my writing, but one in particular stands out—my music.

I play the French horn, and have performed in various groups all my life. I love playing, but there came a time when I realized I had to do something more if I wanted to take the next step in my writing career. I'd been submitting my novels to publishers for years, and though I'd gotten a couple encouraging notes from editors, I still didn't have that coveted publishing contract.

I knew something had to give. That something was my music.

It wasn't an easy decision. Playing music is one of the great joys of my life. I started taking private lessons in first grade, trained all the way through my college years, and in addition to performing, I also taught lessons. But I had to do something, so I made the decision to push toward becoming a published novelist. I told my conductors I was taking a break, knowing full well that down the road, I might not be able to get back into any of the symphonies, pit orchestras or chamber groups where it's rare to find an opening. All would have to name a replacement for me, which meant it was very possible there would be no opening when I was ready to return.

It was a risk, and it was a huge sacrifice, but at the time it was the only answer. As I had hoped, the decision freed up a good amount of time to write, and allowed me to focus intently on that part of my life. I completed more stories, attended several conferences, and submitted like crazy over the next few years. Before I knew it, I had two novels accepted for publication. The sacrifice was worth it.

## Decide What You Really Want

Even if I hadn't gotten published, I wouldn't have regretted my decision, because I had to give my writing every chance to succeed. Fortunately, when I was ready to get back into music, a friend of mine put me in touch with the new symphony conductor, and within a few months, I was back in my old seat as well as playing in a new pit orchestra. Today, I enjoy my music even more than I used to, because I feel like I have a better balance in my life, since my writing career is closer to where I want it to be.

No matter where you are in your creative pursuits, realize sacrifice is always part of the picture. Your days are already full. Something has to give. It's the old story about not being able to have it all. In the game of life, we're the kids in the toy store. I want this, *and* that, *and* that, *and* that! Oh, and what's *that* over there? Unfortunately, it just doesn't work that way. We must set priorities and being able to sacrifice makes that possible. It also helps if you know a little bit about how the human brain naturally resists change.

### Overcome the Brain's Aversion to Loss

Any time you think about making a change in your routine that involves sacrifice (which it often does), your brain is going to resist. The human brain *hates* loss, because loss causes pain.

Imagine a terrible disease has been unleashed on humankind and there are only 600 people left on the planet. A scientist believes he's found a cure, but he has two versions and he leaves the choice up to you. Which would you choose?

1. Cure A is guaranteed to save exactly 200 people.

2. Cure B has a 1/3 probability of saving 600, but a 2/3 probability of saving no one.

In the actual study conducted by two psychologists, most people chose Cure A. You may have noticed that both cures have the same result, but are just framed differently. Cure B focuses on loss, while Cure A focuses on lives saved. More people chose A because the brain can't stand the idea of losing.

This is called "loss aversion," and it affects us all. Losses have a greater psychological impact on us than gains, so we try to avoid losses at all costs, even if the end result means gaining something substantial.

Russell A. Poldrack, a professor of psychology at Stanford University, wrote about this in *Scientific American Mind*. He was involved in a study that monitored the brain activity of people deciding whether or not to take a gamble using real money. As the amount of the reward increased, there was a corresponding enhanced activity in the brain's reward circuitry. Likewise, as the potential losses accrued, that reward circuitry quieted down.

What was most interesting was that the overall brain reaction was *stronger* in response to possible losses than to gains. We can see this in real life when we are faced with losing something. The experience triggers strong emotions, such as stress and anxiety, which can be difficult to deal with. These emotions are more powerful than the happiness or joy that may lie on the other side of that loss. We fight harder to avoid loss than to achieve a gain.

That means when you try to find time for your creative work, you may have a battle ahead of you.

## Fight Brain Cling

As you consider sacrificing something for your writing and you start to imagine how you might shuffle things around, your brain will fight to keep life as it is. That doesn't mean what you have is best, it simply means that you *have it*, and that you are familiar with it.

A few months ago, I came up against this "brain clinging to what you have" phenomenon. It was time to trade in my old Ford Ranger, but my brain fought me on it as I wrestled with the decision I had to make.

The thing is, I was attached to the old truck. It was a beautiful deep blue color with a matching shell, extra-cab and stepside bed. It had a nice 4.0-liter engine and it had taken me over the road for nearly a decade. Yes, a decade, which is why common sense dictated that I needed a new vehicle.

But it was also special because I associated it with my dog, Morrigan, a jet-black German shepherd. She and I went everywhere in that truck, from the time she was a puppy until she passed away at age thirteen. Every time I opened the door she'd leap into her spot in the extra-cab, her brown eyes laughing and her tongue hanging out.

We had a lot of good times in that truck, but one night this aging vehicle left me stranded in the middle of a winter storm in high heels and formal dress. That wasn't fun. Shortly after that, I started having all kinds of trouble with it, and I knew it was time to either pay for a major run of repairs, or trade it in. If I waited too long, more would go wrong while the miles crept up and the value plummeted.

It was a logical and seemingly simple decision, and I even found a new all-wheel-drive vehicle I was excited about, but boy my brain still fought me on it! I did *not* want to let go of the vehicle, the one in which I'd experienced so many good memories. It wasn't easy, but I now love my new vehicle and am busy making new memories.

**Overcome Your Fear of Change**

Adults tend to cling hard to the way things are, even if these things aren't great. But there are other reasons we resist sacrifice and change, even when these two steps lead to a better future. Here's why:

- Fear of the unknown
- Fear we'll make the wrong decision
- Fear of loss
- Doubt in our own abilities
- Desire for a safety net
- Worry we'll be "stuck" with the outcome of our decisions, whether they're good, bad, or both

Psychologists say we hold onto all of our stuff, routines, and habits as a type of safety net. Think of it as security in an unsecure world. Go back to the times in your life when you were facing a change. You may have thought about letting go of something, or changing something, only to become nervous and anxious, spending far too long second-guessing yourself.

This is because (per above) we tend to view whatever we stand to lose as a bigger deal than whatever we stand to gain. Resisting change, however, natural as it is, will keep you stuck exactly where you are.

In the above list, the reasons why we avoid making changes are all rooted in fear, and fear is not the emotion that should guide decision-making. When fear runs the show, the end result is often a negative one. But logical, well-thought-out decisions, as scary as they can be, will make life better.

If I had kept the truck, for example, instead of enjoying the peace of mind that comes with having a reliable vehicle in my garage, I'd be sinking money and time into an old machine, and possibly facing another night stranded alongside the road.

To increase your chances of making the best decision, don't make it based on fear or resistance, or on your brain's tendency to cling to what you have. Realize how your brain works, and be willing to take a leap of faith based on your own best judgment.

Time Treasure

## Let Go

List the habits and routines you're clinging to right now that are stopping you from getting creative work done. Do this by reviewing your daily routines as if you were a time auditor. Determine which activities are truly helpful and which can be sacrificed to make room for your creative dream.

Ask yourself: What activity or habit can I let go of to free up more time? To make this simpler, imagine you're twelve years old and able to just change your schedule, willy nilly, purely for fun. How would you do it?

**While in that frame of mind, write down the three things in your typical weekly routine you could give up right now to make time for your writing:**

1. _____
2. _____
3. _____

Don't be surprised if completing this list makes you nervous. That's your brain doing its thing. To help make it easier, take small steps. You don't have to give up all three things today, but take on one this week, and add the others in subsequent weeks. It's like buying an expensive gift on layaway. You invest small amounts now for the bigger reward later.

> When I first thought about giving up my truck, I didn't trade it in right then. I asked friends for their advice and also started looking around for another vehicle. When you begin to think about giving something up, talk to your friends and play out the possible consequences and outcomes. Imagine how it will feel to have more time to write. Zero in on only the good feelings that will come with what you hope to gain, and downplay the brain's overreaction to what you need to give up.
>
> Then, just "let it go." It will feel funny at first, but once you have the time to create, you'll know you made the right decision.

# PART II

# INCREASE PRODUCTIVITY TO EXPAND YOUR WRITING TIME

So far, you've learned about the many things that can make you feel rushed and overwhelmed, and like you have no time for your writing. You've abandoned the myth of the "perfect writing life," shut down your distractions, reduced the number of decisions you have to make each day, and sacrificed another activity to make more time to write.

Congratulations! These significant changes will allow you to fit more creative time into your schedule, and to get back to feeling like an on-purpose artist. Now it's time to ramp up your productivity so you can get more done throughout the day, and thus further expand your writing time.

In the next several chapters, I give you a bunch of productivity tips or "hacks," if you will, to help you do just that. The more productive you are at work and at home, the more you'll get done, and the more time you'll have to do whatever you like—in this case, to write!

But first, I need to ask an important question: Why do you want more time to write? Take a few minutes right now to think about your answer, because it's important. It forms the basis of all the decisions you will make from now on about your writing.

## Your Key Motivation: More Time to Write

The following strategy will help you to fully explore your motivations for carving out more time to write. To start, set a timer for five minutes, and then ask yourself, "Why do I want more time to write?" Jot down whatever comes to mind. When you run out of answers, ask yourself "why" again.

For example, my first answer might be, "I want to find more time to write so I can finish my novel." *Why?* "To fulfill my dream of holding my book in my hands." *Why?* "Because that would make me feel I had reached my goal." *Why is that important?* "Because it would show that I had created something from my heart and shared it with the world."

You get the idea. Hold a mini question-and-answer session with yourself to get to the core reason why you want more time to write.

Spend the full five minutes asking and answering the question, "Why?" Do it right now. If you need more space, use your own notebook.

_____

_____

_____

_____

_____

Now let's look at your answers. Maybe you talked about how

much you enjoy writing, how it's always been a dream of yours to hold your book in your hands, or how you feel most at home when you're writing. Maybe you consider writing a calling, and something you're compelled to do, and you feel restless and uneasy when you don't get enough time to do it.

Whatever your answer, hold onto it, because we'll return to it in a minute. Now, I have a second question for you:

*How will you feel ten years from now if you fail to find the extra time to write?*

Again, set the timer for five minutes, and follow the same instructions as above. My answer to this question might be, "I'll feel like I let myself down."

After your answer, follow up with another question: *How will that make you feel?* In my case, the answer would be: "That I wasn't strong enough to go after my dreams, or wasn't disciplined enough."

_____
_____
_____
_____
_____

If you wrote that you'll feel sad, angry, or depressed, or like you let yourself down, it's important to consider those feelings carefully. You may have imagined that ten years from now, if you don't find more time to write, your life will look much the same as it does at this moment, and that is likely to make you unhappy.

Now take a look at both sets of answers. As you re-read them, pull out the key words that describe how you feel and record them in the two columns below. In the column on the left, write the key words from your first answer, and on the right, those from your second answer.

My key words:

| Why do I want to find more time to write? | How will I feel if I don't? |
|---|---|
| Finish novel | Let myself down |
| My dream | Not strong enough |
| Book in my hands | Missed out |
| Reached my goal | Lost opportunities |
| Created something | Unfulfilled dreams |
| Put it out into the world | Let life pass me by |

You get the idea. Your key words:

| Why do I want to find more time to write? | How will I feel if I don't? |
|---|---|
|  |  |
|  |  |
|  |  |
|  |  |
|  |  |
|  |  |

Now take a look at your chart. What do you think?

## Post This Chart Where You Can See It

This exercise should make it clear in very immediate terms what your writing means to you, and how you will feel in the future if you don't make more time for it in the present. Post your chart where you can see it every day, such as on the refrigerator or near the bathroom sink, to help remind you of your commitment.

Seeing the chart should help you keep your daily tasks in perspective. You have to get groceries and exercise and go to work and get the car fixed when it breaks down and chauffeur the kids and a billion other things. Your brain is wired to focus on the tasks of daily living, which is why you need reminders about the bigger things you want to accomplish—like writing. By exposing yourself over and over again to your priorities, you can gradually program your brain to think of your writing as being just as important as keeping the refrigerator stocked. This is critical for one huge reason:

> We show what we value in life not by what we think or say, but by what we do.

That means if you're not already finding enough time to write in your daily schedule, you're telling your brain, your family, your friends, your spirit, and your god (if you have one) that writing is not that important to you. Even if you *feel* writing is important, or tell others that it's important, if you're not taking action to back it up, life forces will conspire to keep you from writing.

That may sound a little twilight zone-y to you, but the truth is that your actions reveal what really matters. Examine what you currently spend the most time doing, and what you're investing yourself in. If writing isn't near the top of that list, and it *is* a priority, it's time to make some changes.

CHAPTER 5

# PRIORITIZE

I'M A BIG fan of lists. If I need to get something done, I write it down. It helps me to keep track of the various tasks that need to be completed in my life, and plus, it just feels really good to cross something off when it's finished. Then I know I've at least accomplished something that day.

Whether you actually write down the things you have to do or not, you have a "to-do" list, too. It could be in your head, on your smartphone calendar app, or on your computer, but somewhere, you have a list. Take a moment now to consider what's on that list. Try to count the number of items, including the things you have to do on a daily basis, and those that are waiting in the wings for when you get time to address them. I'm not talking about eating breakfast or getting dressed, but about those things you need to do, like "finish X project at work" or "get the clothes to the dry cleaners" or "meet with Johnny's teacher about his math scores."

Like most people, your to-do list may be sort of like the soap scum in your bathtub. Whatever doesn't get "rinsed away" today goes on tomorrow's list, and whatever doesn't get "rinsed away" tomorrow goes on the next day's list, and the darned thing builds up like that ring around your tub until it's not much more than an eyesore. You come to the end of each day with so many things left undone that all you feel is defeated.

There's a name for this phenomenon: it's called the "Zeigarnik effect," named after Bluma Zeigarnik. She was a Lithuanian psychologist and researcher who discovered that we have a tendency to remember more clearly those tasks we *haven't* finished over the tasks we have. If you've ever heard of the saying, "one aw shucks wipes out a thousand attaboys," you know what I'm talking about here. Even if you get a ton of things done and leave only one thing unfinished, you'll probably feel like you didn't accomplish what you were supposed to.

Zeigarnik's interesting experiment consisted of asking people to complete a series of different tasks. They solved puzzles, for example, or assembled flat-pack boxes. They were allowed to complete some of the tasks, but were interrupted and pulled away before they finished others. Afterward, Zeigarnik interviewed all the participants, and found that they were able to recall details of the interrupted tasks about *ninety percent better* than those they had been allowed to complete.

Ninety percent!

This tells you that whatever you feel has been left unfinished in your day is going to bug you. It may keep you up at night, and cause you to completely ignore everything that you *did* get done. It's just how the brain works.

This can be dangerous. If you feel that just about every day you are unable to keep up, the stress is going to become chronic. That's not only bad for your health, it's bad for your creativity. Yet this is what's happening to many of you who are reading this book. You may feel like you often come to the end of the day with too many things still left undone. If one of those things is your writing, you'll probably feel even worse.

If you imagine the answer is to increase productivity and efficiency so you can finish off that entire to-do list, think again.

## Abandon the Idea that You Can Do More and More And More...

On the one hand, yes, there are things you can do to increase your productivity, and I'm going to talk about some of those things in a minute. But, on the other hand, there's only so much you can do in a day. You have just twenty-four hours, and you can't add more no matter how much you might like to. You're not a machine, and you need to be sure you have time to take care of yourself—to eat nutritious food, sleep, exercise, and enjoy some downtime.

The answer is not to figure out how to do more and more and more and more…because somewhere along the way, you're going to burn out and collapse. That's why the first, most important and most effective productivity tip is this:

### KWIT: Keep What's Important on Top

It's time to kwit all the stuff that's just not that important. Kwit worrying about whether or not you have homemade treats to serve at your child's birthday party. Kwit killing yourself at work trying to make everything perfect. Kwit taking on extra projects you don't really need to do. Kwit saying yes to everyone. Kwit trying to do everything yourself.

You have my permission to KWIT!

## How to KWIT

Starting today, split your to-do list in half. On the top half, write three—and only three—major things you need to accomplish today. (One of them should be your writing.) So for example:

- Spend thirty minutes writing.
- Finish X project at work.
- Take Jimmy to the museum.

Then draw a horizontal line, and underneath, list the other less important things you'd "like" to do if you get time to do them. For example:

- Take the clothes to the dry cleaners.
- Call the plumber to fix the dripping faucet.
- Take the car to the garage to get an oil change.

This method makes you *prioritize* those things that are really important to you. It also helps you take the pressure off of yourself. You probably have a lot of things "waiting in the wings" that need to get done, like cleaning out the garage, replacing the washing machine, donating old stuff in the house, framing some important pictures, updating computer apps and programs, making an eye doctor appointment, etc.

The problem is, if you add these to a long to-do list and then don't get everything crossed off, you'll be stuck in the Zeigarnik effect, focusing on the undone tasks and causing yourself way too much stress in the process.

With this new list, you create a situation where you can accomplish your priorities and feel good about them whether you finish the rest or not.

You may have already tried something like this before. Certainly you've heard it's important to set priorities. But then somehow you got wrapped up in all those other little things you had to do and your priorities went out the window. Let's look at why that happens.

## Three Priority Killers

There are three main reasons why you may fail to prioritize your tasks, even though you know better:

1. Busy work
2. Time scarcity mindset
3. Fear

### 1. Busy Work is Easier

The little things like checking your emails, updating social media posts, putting the dishes away, picking up the living room, organizing files, cleaning your desk, updating your accounts, etc., get in the way of your priorities. Yes, all this stuff needs to get done eventually, but instead of scheduling an hour or so to attend to it, it's easier to fritter away your time doing a little here and there throughout the day. This robs time from your bigger projects like writing, submitting stories to publishers, or creating a marketing plan.

We waste time on these smaller tasks even when the bigger priorities are more important to us for one reason: it's easier to do the small stuff. A 2014 survey from AtTask and Harris Poll reported that U.S. employees spend only about forty-five percent of their day on primary job duties—less than half! The rest is spent on email, meetings, administrative tasks, and interruptions.

Researchers have also found that we are actually happiest at work when performing these minimal tasks: "With rote work, you get a feeling of accomplishment, but you haven't exerted a lot of mental activity," study author Gloria Mark of the University of California, Irvine, told the *Wall Street Journal*. "It gives you a feeling of fulfillment, but there's not frustration or stress."

This is why sitting down to write incites the urge to clean the dishes or do a load of laundry. These tasks are easy and accomplishing them gives us the impression we're being productive. We're not being lazy, we're answering emails!

The truth is that we actually *are* being lazy, just a little bit. I tend to fall into this trap especially when the writing gets hard. My brain rebels, and I'm off to check emails, clean the bathroom, or feed the cat. It's a classic case of going easy on myself and doing the simpler task.

In a typical day in your life, when might you be guilty of this?

**2. Time-Scarcity Mindset**

There is a general trend in today's culture to imagine that we never have enough time. People say it often: "I don't have time." We have programmed ourselves to believe that time is scarce, which may seem like no big deal. Most of us *do* feel like we're constantly running out of time.

But the danger is that the more you tell yourself this message, the more you believe it's true. That puts you in a constant "stress state," which tanks your decision-making skills. Being stressed out because you feel like you don't have enough time means you're probably running from task to task feeling uptight and making split-second decisions. That increases your risk of neglecting your writing time in favor of putting out fires.

A Harvard economist compared people who were poor with busy professionals who felt they were always crunched for time. He found startling similarities between the two. Both groups fell into the trap of thinking they "didn't have enough," which is sort of a panic-type psychology. That causes the desire for survival to kick in, which leads to making decisions that may be beneficial in the short-term, but sabotage long-term goals. Farmers in India, for example, were better planners and thinkers when they had enough cash from their crops. When their coffers were empty, they focused only on short-term gains. That helped them save some money initially, but robbed them of earnings later on.

People who feel like they are always out of time tend to do the same thing. Writers are really good at this. If you feel like you don't have the time to write today, you tell yourself you'll do it tomorrow. The short-term gain is that you have more time today to do the other things you think are important, but in the long run, your writing progress suffers.

It's a lot like being too busy to renew your car registration. You plan to do it in the morning, but when you're late for work, you blow it off. You try again Wednesday, but something comes up, so you put it off until the next day. Soon the license plate is expired, and that causes you to worry about being pulled over and fined, so you drive in a hyper-vigilant state. Suddenly this small task has become a much larger problem, causing stress, and potentially robbing you of more time than it would have taken to renew the registration before it expired.

"That's at the heart of the scarcity trap," researcher Sendhil Mullainathan told *NPR*. "You are so focused on the urgent that the important gets waylaid. But because the important gets waylaid, you're experiencing even more scarcity tomorrow."

If you think this whole idea of time scarcity is merely a by-product of today's world and not a personal problem, consider this: In 1979, professor emeritus at the Free University in Amsterdam Bob Goudzwaard wrote about "scarcity of time" in his book, *Capitalism and Progress*.

"Nearly everyone in western society suffers from a frightful shortage of time," he wrote. "This lack of time is apparent not only from the quick tempo of our lives and from our crowded schedules, but also from the manner in which the modern family spends its time."

Remember—this was long before smartphones, and even before most people had computers in their homes, and still people felt pressed for time. So it's not necessarily modern-day technology that's causing you to feel this way (though of course it doesn't help).

Instead, it could just be how you're looking at things. To empower yourself, realize that the "time-scarcity mindset" is one that you can change.

## 3. Fear

You'll know fear is sabotaging your priorities when you have fifteen minutes of free time, and your first thought is, "Oh sweet, I could work on chapter ten!" And your second thought is, "Well, no, I've only got fifteen minutes. I'm not going to be able to get much done in that short amount of time."

Gong. Thank you for playing, but you just lost to fear. That second thought had nothing to do with time and everything to do with fear—fear of the blank page, or of not being good enough to finish the chapter, or of not being able to live up to the challenge that writing presents every day.

Each time you have a few minutes to write and you don't write, it's not because you failed to prioritize, but because you gave in to fear. You may be afraid that you won't be able to accomplish what you want to accomplish in that time, so you end up psyching yourself out. It's a perfectly natural reaction. We all care about our writing or we wouldn't be writers. Most writers I know share a seat with this sort of fear just about every day. You just need to overcome it so you don't lose that precious time to get some words down.

**Get Past the Three Priority Killers**

To get past these three priority killers—busy work, the time scarcity mindset, and fear—follow the suggestions in each of the time treasures below. These are simple changes you can make each day that will help ensure your priorities get your attention first.

---

Time Treasure

## KWIT

To avoid time-sucking busywork, keep what's important on top. Do your most difficult project early in the day when your mind is fresh and you have the most energy. Energy fuels your productivity and willpower, leaving you less vulnerable to distractions. Accomplish something major in the morning and everything else will feel easier from that point on. Plus, by starting your day in this productive way, you'll naturally up your game for the rest of the day, as well.

Many authors write first thing in the morning because writing is a difficult task, mentally and creatively. Tackling it first makes it more likely that it will get done and also creates a great sense of accomplishment that sustains you. It's a motivating strategy.

To help you zero in on what's important to you, set three priorities each for tomorrow, next week, next month, and next year. Then tackle those priorities before allowing your time to go to other tasks. Here's an example:

*Next day priorities*

1. Write 500 words.
2. Get report done for work.
3. Attend Suzie's soccer game.

*Weekly priorities*

1. Finish chapter three.
2. Exercise at least three hours over the course of the week.
3. Spend at least two hours of quality time with my kids.

*Monthly priorities*

1. Attend a writer's conference.
2. Research and identify at least two publishers for my book.

3. Find a plumber to fix the faucet.

*Yearly priorities*

1. Finish my book.

2. Submit it to at least one contest.

3. Lose five pounds.

When you accomplish three things in each time frame, you'll feel motivated to do even more. Keep setting your three priorities as you go, and that frantic feeling of stress will gradually dissipate.

---

Time Treasure

## **Regain Control of Your Time**

What's the solution to the time scarcity trap? Fortunately, there are a few of them.

- **Change your messages to yourself.** Instead of telling yourself, "I don't have time!", say, "I have the time, and it's my choice how to spend it." This puts the power back in your court, which helps reduce stress. Since most stress is caused by feeling out of control, the second you reclaim your power over time, you'll feel better. This new state of mind will also help you make better decisions that will lead to having more free time down the road.

- **Schedule at least two thirty-minute blocks of time per day to do nothing.** These time blocks are called "blank times" or "white times," and should be used to enjoy a stress-relieving activity, or to catch up on things. Don't pack your day with back-to-back appointments. Leave some white space in your calendar.

- **Schedule a "catch-up day."** At least once every two weeks (more often if you can), set aside a day to catch up. This is the day when you can attend to all the things you haven't had time to do. When you know that day is scheduled, you can relax a bit more about things that aren't getting done, knowing you will have the time to get to them soon.

- **Give some time away.** Say your son wants to play catch, or a friend needs someone to talk to. Instead of stressing about how you don't have time, take fifteen minutes and give it away. It will benefit your relationships and help you overcome the "time-scarcity" mindset. Doing this sends the message to your brain that you do, indeed, have time to spare.

- **Spend time doing something you enjoy.** At least once a week, make a point to spend time doing something you enjoy. It doesn't matter what as long as it gives something back to you. This can help you feel more in control of your time, and encourages positive emotions, which are connected to higher productivity.

- **Schedule time to reflect.** Every day or at the very least once a week, pause for at least an hour and reflect on how you spend your time. Ask yourself if you are spending it well, or if you're wasting it. Take a walk, meditate, journal, go for a drive, or engage in some other activity that will allow your mind to mull this over and formulate a plan for how you'd like to change anything in the coming week.

- **Let things go.** There are *always* going to be tasks that don't get done. Rather than bemoan that fact, accept instead that it's okay. Don't stress over what you can't change as long as you're spending time on what's important to you.

---

Time Treasure

## Face the Fear

To become a more productive writer, you have to face the fear. You already knew that, but it's a lot easier said than done. That means you need to put a few safeguards in place in your brain.

1. **Go with your first impulse no matter what.** When you have a few free minutes and you get the impulse to

write, do it, no matter what other thoughts erupt in your mind. Make it a rule to follow that initial impulse. Trust your first gut desire, and don't allow fearful thoughts to take that time away from you.

2. **Learn to live with fear.** Realize that this is normal. All writers and creative artists deal with it all the time. We have to learn to live with fear, while not allowing it to control us. Accept your fearful feelings and write anyway, whenever you get a moment to do it.

3. **Allow the writing to be less than perfect.** We're going to talk more about perfectionism in a later chapter, but for now let me suggest that you allow yourself to write badly. Often our fear of the page comes from being afraid to write a less than perfect set of paragraphs, but the beauty of writing is that we can always fix it later. Just get something down that you can work with.

### Remember What's Important

Everyone gets busy, and life can seem crazy at times. That's why it's critical to keep what's important on top, because the rest of the day can so easily get away from you. Keep your writing as a priority in your mind, every day. Get it done first if you can, and if not, schedule another time that's not easy to skip.

As for all that other stuff? Give yourself permission to KWIT.

CHAPTER 6

# ARREST YOUR TIME THIEVES

WHAT ARE THE hidden destroyers of any writer's best intentions? Time thieves—those sneaky little activities that feel harmless, but steal your time right out from under you. They're incredibly destructive because they gobble up precious minutes that you'll never get back. When they're tiptoeing through your life, snatching half an hour here for Facebook, an hour there for TV, it doesn't seem that big a deal. But add up all the minutes lost over a period of a year and you could be looking at a seriously large number—one that would have given you a novel if you'd been writing instead.

That's the bad news. The good news? You can take control of this situation. You can increase productivity by identifying your time thieves and creating a new security system that keeps them from robbing you of those precious minutes you so desperately need.

## THE TIME THIEVES

### Television

An astonishing eighty percent of American adults watch three-and-a-half hours of TV per day—which takes up about half of their leisure time, according to a 2015 survey by the Bureau of Labor Statistics (BLS). A 2014 Nielsen media ratings report put the number even higher, stating the average American watches five hours per day. That's not just a huge time thief; it's also horrible for your health. A 2015 study found that the more television people watched, the more likely they were to die prematurely.

Examine what you're watching and how much time it's taking. There's nothing wrong with sitting down to relax now and then, but if you want to be more productive, find the "off" button and use it more often. Better yet, schedule your viewing time around your favorite shows, and then turn the TV off when they're over. Don't fall for those teasers that try to lure you into watching the next show.

**How many hours a day do you spend (on average) watching television?**

_____ **hours per day**

### Social Media

Social media networking now accounts for nearly thirty percent of the time Americans spend on the Internet—an average of 1.72 hours a day, according to a 2015 report from the Global Web Index. That doesn't include blogging, reading blogs, or online research, just social media interaction.

It may be hard to imagine that so much of your day is spent on social media, but take a second look. A 2015 report from Informate Mobile Intelligence revealed that people check Facebook, Twitter, and other accounts an average of seventeen times a day—once every waking hour. And the highest usage wasn't in the "kids" group —it was in the 25-54 age bracket!

Facebook reported in 2016 that users spent an average of fifty minutes a day (nearly an hour) on Facebook, Instagram, and Messenger platforms. That may not seem like much until you remember that you have twenty-four hours a day, and about eight are spent sleeping and another eight working. That leaves just eight hours, and the average Facebook user shoots one of them on the social media site.

To keep social media from gobbling up your time, set limits on when you allow yourself to check it. Dedicate thirty minutes a day, for example, or every other day, or on certain days of the week. Be vigilant about stopping on time, so you don't fall victim to the "just one more thing" trick the social media thief uses to keep you from breaking away.

You can also check social media as a "reward" during the day, as long as you keep it to no more than ten minutes. This so-called "grazing" used as a reward *between completed projects* actually increased productivity in the workplace by about nine percent, according to one study. Think of checking social media as the modern-day "smoke break." Just don't let it take over your day.

*Note*: Face-to-face interactions increased productivity even more than social media breaks, so consider getting up and talking to a colleague or friend for ten minutes instead!

## How many hours a day do you spend (on average) logged into social media?

_____ **hours per day**

**Email**

Think about how many emails you receive a day. The average corporate worker gets about eighty-four, according to a report from the Radicati technology market research firm in California. Now think about how much time you spend answering all those emails. For the average worker, it takes up about a quarter of the day (2.6 hours, or thirteen hours a week, according to a 2012 report by the McKinsey Global Institute). Answering emails was the second most time-consuming activity in the workday, outside of tasks to complete (aka "doing your job").

Set specific times during the day to deal with email. Three times a day (with set time limits) is average. The rest of the time, quit the program! To further dissuade this time thief, try these tips:

- Think about the email newsletters you've signed up for. When one comes into your inbox, ask yourself if it's adding value to your day. If not, unsubscribe.

- Think twice about creating folders. You may have read that it helps make you more organized in responding, but recent research questions that approach, and states that using the "search" function to find what you need may be more effective. You can also save important emails in a project folder outside of your email program. It will lighten your inbox, while keeping emails where you need them—with your project.

- Try applications like Toggl.com and RescueTime to track the time you spend on email. You'll be surprised at how much of a time thief email can be.

- Quit or log out of your email program when you're not using it, or use apps like "Inbox Pause" to keep new emails from interrupting you.

- Don't make checking email your first priority. It's difficult to resist the urge to check email first thing, but if you accomplish something more important instead, you'll start the day motivated and will remain more productive all day long. Don't allow email to steal time from your priorities.

**How many hours a day do you spend (on average) reading and responding to emails?**

_____ hours per day

**Requests from Others**

You may have trouble saying "no" when you need to. I'll be helping you more with that in Chapter 9, but for now, realize that requests from others are time thieves. You may enjoy doing the tasks others ask you to do, which is okay. Just check in with yourself to see how many requests a week you're saying "yes" to, and whether or not you're happy with the results.

Remember your priorities, and don't let the needs of others keep you from getting them done. Replying to requests with a simple, "I can't, I'm sorry," should suffice. (See Chapter 9 for more tips.)

**How many hours a day do you spend (on average) doing things for others that don't contribute to your purpose?**

_____ hours per day

### Interruptions

You're working away on your project, and someone knocks on the door. You look up, address what that person wants, and then go back to your project. Don't be surprised if you stare at the screen for a while before being able to get going again.

Interruptions are costly. They increase errors, cause you to take longer to finish a task, and boost stress. A key 2014 study from George Mason University found that people who were interrupted while writing produced poorer quality essays than those who worked undisturbed. Other research has found that it can take an average of *twenty-three minutes* to recover lost concentration.

To minimize interruptions:

- **Communicate clearly.** To work or write uninterrupted, make it clear to others that you don't want to be disturbed. Close your door. Don't answer the phone or check emails. Hang a "do not disturb" sign. Whatever it takes.

- **Don't answer the phone or the door.** When unexpected visitors come calling, avoid any interaction at all, or at the very least, apologize and reschedule the visit.

- **Turn off your cell phone**, or at least silence it.

- **Isolate yourself**—go somewhere you won't be disturbed.

**How many hours a day (on average) do interruptions steal? (Make your best guess based on the fact that each interruption costs you about twenty-five minutes.)**

_____ **hours per day**

## Commuting Time

The average one-way commute in America today is 25.5 minutes, according to the Census Bureau's annual American Community Survey (2011), and it's getting longer. Compared with commuting times in the year 2000, today's times are higher.

An hour a day is a lot of stolen time. Instead of letting this time thief rob you, try these tips:

- **Listen to audio books:** They're a great way to "absorb" different voices and the rhythm of language. You can also listen to audiobooks about the writing craft, or those that help you research a current project.

- **"Write" on the go:** Use your smartphone or digital voice recorder to talk out plot problems, character traits, or your next book description. Many writers "write" their blog posts this way. Bonus: there are several apps that convert voice recorder data to text. Apps like "Voice Assistant" also let you post updates to social media without typing, and the Dragon software transcribes your audio to text.

- **Brainstorm:** Take advantage of the automatic task of driving to brainstorm your next project, or to look for solutions to your current one. Keep your voice recorder nearby so you can make note of any ideas that come to you.

- **Edit:** When taking the bus or train, or carpooling, use your time to edit what you've already written. Print the pages out and take them with you.

## How many hours a day do you spend (on average) commuting?

_____ hours per day

### 7. Fatigue/Lack of Sleep

If you're tired, your productivity will suffer. Less than seven hours of sleep results in poor performance. Six hours or less is bad for your health, creativity, and productivity.

Set regular sleep and wake times and stick to them. Exercise every day so you feel tired at bedtime, and turn off all electronic gadgets at least an hour before you retire. See Chapter 13 for more tips.

## How many days a week do you fail to get seven to eight hours of sleep?

_____ days

## Other Time Thieves that May Be Stealing from You

You may have other time thieves in your life that aren't listed here. Some good examples include playing video or smartphone games; reading online media, blogs, or websites for too long; shopping online; spending time doing activities you don't enjoy; attending unnecessary meetings; obsessing over unimportant tasks; standing in line at the supermarket during busy times, etc.

Think about your schedule for a moment, and identify any other time thieves you've discovered, along with estimates of about how much time they're stealing from you per day. Write them down below.

A. _____ Est. hours: _____

B. _____ Est. hours: _____

C. _____ Est. hours: _____

D. _____ Est. hours: _____

E. _____ Est. hours: _____

Now, add up your hours lost to all the time thieves listed above. Add at least a half-hour for each day that you fail to get seven to eight hours of sleep.

Average daily hours lost: _____

Multiply that times seven to get your average number of hours lost per week.

Average weekly hours lost: _____

Next, multiply that number by fifty-two to get your average number of hours lost per year:

Average yearly hours lost: _____

### Time Treasure

## Create a New Weekly Calendar

Seeing these figures in black and white can open your eyes to how much of your time is going down the drain, compelling you to use your hours more wisely.

Compiling all this data won't help, however, if you don't make changes. Begin by setting schedules for checking social media, reading and answering emails, watching television, and any other activities that you determined to be time thieves. Decide which time-wasting activities you need to limit or get rid of entirely, and take action to make sure they don't continue to steal from you.

Start today by rearranging your schedule. It's okay if it doesn't work out perfectly the first week. You can continue to adjust it as needed in the future. By taking this step right now, you can't help but free up some time for writing or writing-related tasks.

CHAPTER 7

# FOCUS FASTER

IMAGINE YOU'VE JUST sat down with thirty minutes to write. You've sequestered yourself in a quiet room during your lunch hour where you won't be disturbed. You've turned off your cell phone and email program to limit distractions, and you're looking forward to some quality creative time. You get a paragraph done, but then you're not sure what should come next. You pause.

Your thoughts wander. You remember your brother's birthday is coming up, and make a mental note to get a card. You stare at the screen, find something wrong with the last sentence you wrote, and fix it. You reach for your phone to look something up, but realize this would be a distraction and put it back down.

Fifteen minutes pass. You do your best to focus on the story, but then realize you're feeling chilled. Your sweater is out in the car, but you'd have to break your concentration to go get it. You write another couple sentences and suddenly a door slams down the hall. You look up, wondering what that was. You consider getting up to check, but when you hear nothing further, you decide to continue writing. It's difficult, though. Your concentration wavers. Soon, your time is up. As you look back at your work, you realize you wrote only two paragraphs.

What went wrong here? One very big thing: you failed to focus on your story, and it just cost you that thirty minutes you worked so hard to set aside. Maybe if you'd had an hour you would have done better, but that's not always possible. That's why this chapter is called "focus faster." You not only need to be able to focus well to become a more productive writer, but you must get into that focusing mode as quickly as you can.

## Retrain Your Brain

We aren't as good at focusing, or concentrating, as we used to be. I see this in my music students. Whereas focused attention used to be something everyone learned in school, now it's something I have to really work on with my kids during their music lessons. To sit down and practice for thirty minutes at a time is something that many children and adolescents just find excruciating these days.

Adults are in the same boat, finding it more and more difficult to drop into a focused state or to sustain that focus for any length of time. Technology is a big part of the problem. Gadgets provide endless distractions, and our brains are wired to respond. Those beeps, flashes, and vibrations promise a sort of reward the brain likes. A note from a friend, a retweet of a post, or a comment on a blog are all like chocolate for the brain, and we've gotten so we crave them, which makes it even more difficult to focus on something else.

One study of 300 middle school, high school, and college students revealed that participants were able to focus and stay on task for an average of only three minutes! Even when they shut down the gadgets, the students were "thinking" about the distractions, wondering if someone had responded to a post on Facebook, for example, or if they'd received a text back from a friend.

Technology giant Microsoft recently surveyed 2,000 participants and studied the brain activity of 112 others to gather data about our ability to focus. They reported that the human attention span had fallen from twelve seconds in the year 2000 to eight seconds today. Goldfish, on the other hand, have been found in studies to be able to pay attention for nine seconds. (Gulp. Or should I say, glub?) The researchers blamed technology and smartphones.

We live in a world now where technology is always on our minds. It's made focus more difficult, and that's not good news, because focusing wasn't easy to begin with.

## It's About Tuning Out

When you think about focusing on your story, you may imagine that it's all about how well you can tune into the characters, setting, and dialogue. The truth is, however, that focus is not about your ability to *tune in* to your story, but your ability to *tune out* everything else.

You've probably experienced those writing sessions where you were completely absorbed in what you were doing, and when you looked up at the clock, you were shocked at how much time had passed. You were in the "flow," your mind completely focused on what you were doing. This is the peak creative state, and one you want to get to as often and as quickly as you can, because that's when you get the most and the best work done.

How do we get to this flow state more often? There's a part of the brain called the "ventrolateral prefrontal cortex (VLPFC)" that fires up when you need to inhibit a natural response—like a distraction. Let's say you're writing away and your cell phone buzzes (because you failed to turn it off…hint hint). If you planned to focus on writing, your VLPFC will go to work inhibiting your natural response, which is to respond to the buzzing. Depending on how well it works, you'll either go on writing or succumb to the impulse to check your phone.

This area also works to inhibit emotional and muscle responses. It's like your brain's braking system, stopping you from doing things you would automatically do. Scientists have discovered that the better your VLPFC works, the better you are at focusing on a task.

In other words, your ability to *stop yourself from responding to distractions*, no matter where they come from, determines your ability to focus and concentrate. I'll take it a step further and say that your ability to tune out distractions determines how much you'll accomplish during your writing time.

It doesn't sound too difficult, until you try it and find that your brain keeps drifting to other thoughts. Don't be too hard on yourself. The brain's braking system isn't the most hearty of systems. It's not easy to avoid your natural compulsions, as anyone on a diet faced with a dozen donuts will attest.

## Focus Challenges

Technology is definitely a factor in reducing our ability to focus, but it's not the only one. There are a number of issues that can make it harder to concentrate on your writing or anything else. Things like decision fatigue, stress, interruptions, multi-tasking, and lack of exercise will all make the brain's braking system less effective. Then if you add on other distractions around you, like the television blaring, the phone ringing, people talking nearby, distracting noises, or even if you're hungry or thirsty, you'll be more inclined to succumb to your impulses and your focus will go out the window.

Age is another factor affecting the VLPFC, and I'm not talking only about seniors. *Just like the rest of the body, the brain slows down with age.* When the fine lines start showing up around your eyes and the gray hairs make their appearance, that's about the time your brain starts changing, too. Beginning at the age of twenty, we start to gradually lose brain cells, which slows processing speed. According to a 2014 study, starting at age twenty-four, cognitive abilities start to decline, and about every fifteen years after that, cognitive speed drops by fifteen percent.

Age also means that you start to lose your ability to retain information—it doesn't 'stick" as well. (What did you say your name was?) This can happen as early as your thirties. It may also take you longer to learn new things. As you go on, the cortex gets thinner, and the protective sheath around the neurons starts to degrade. By the age of sixty, the brain actually starts to shrink.

You can fight these factors by taking steps to keep your brain as healthy as possible (exercise regularly, eat well, and keep challenging yourself). In the meantime, though, it's important to realize that as you age, keeping your attention on your task of writing can become more difficult, and you must help yourself to make it easier.

## Make It Easier On Your Brain

You can begin to see why it can be so hard to focus, but it's critical not only to getting your writing done, but to being more productive on the whole. Any time you let your attention drift from any task, you lengthen the amount of time it takes to complete it, and you can't afford to lose time.

You must find ways to increase your ability to concentrate, and in today's hurried world, you can't be slow about it. If it takes you fifteen minutes to get into your writing project, that's fifteen minutes you lost.

The first key to focusing faster is to make it easier for your brain to tune out everything else but the project you're working on. That means you need to **turn everything off.** Don't fool yourself that you can concentrate with your Internet, email, and cell phone accessible, or with the television blaring. Turn them all off. This may be difficult to do at first, but if you stick with it, it will start to become second nature to turn things off when you need to concentrate.

Next, **isolate yourself.** Yes, you can find ways to focus around other people if you have to, but it's harder for your brain. If you don't have a quiet room you can use, get creative. When I worked for a corporation, I used to write in the back stairway. You'd be surprised how few times I was interrupted. Despite all the research on exercise being good for health, most people still prefer the elevator!

If you absolutely can't isolate yourself and you're dealing with noise, **use noise-cancelling headphones**. They can be a great investment in your productivity and writing time. You can also **use music.** It doesn't work for everyone, but it can help some people to shut out distractions and concentrate. Choose something that is relaxing, not stimulating or intense. Music may also help you to more quickly sink into your scene if you choose something that fits with the mood of that scene.

Next, **keep a notebook handy.** Thoughts come up, and one of the best ways to get rid of them so they don't destroy your focus is to write them down. Say you're working on Chapter 9 and suddenly remember that you have to attend an important meeting the next morning. Write it down so you can address it later. Doing so frees up your brain to focus on your task.

To keep hunger from interrupting you, keep some snacks handy, but make sure they're made up of **the right foods.** You may start out focusing well on your project, but if you tank up on donuts and brownies you're going to find your energy flagging fast. Be smart about your snack choices and go for high protein and low sugar. Nuts, whole-wheat crackers, fruits and veggies, yogurt, dark chocolate, and green tea are all great options for energizing your brain and helping you maintain your concentration.

Make sure you have a **glass of water nearby**, too. Even if you're only slightly dehydrated, you may experience symptoms like mild headache, fatigue, and cravings for unhealthy foods that will destroy your concentration. A 2012 study found that being just a little low on your fluid stores could alter your mood, energy level, and ability to think clearly.

These steps will make it easier for your brain to focus quickly and to maintain that focus for the duration of the time you have to write.

## Learn About Chunking

Time management expert and author of the international bestseller *The Pomodoro Technique*, Francesco Cirillo, is credited with coming up with the idea of chunking. He called it "The Pomodoro Technique," named after the tomato-shaped timer he used to track his work as a university student. Others have talked about this technique, as well, and used various names for it, but the principle remains the same.

The idea is that by performing focused work in chunks of time, and then taking breaks in between to restore your mental and physical energy, you are able to focus faster and more intensely. Let's take your writing time as an example.

To chunk it, set a timer for twenty-five minutes, and then write until the timer goes off. Ignore any distracting thoughts and continue to bring your mind back to your task. Once your time is over, take a short break to get up and get a cup of coffee or tea, take a brief walk, or simply spend some time looking out the window, before returning for another chunk of writing.

Continue this way for about four different chunks, followed by a longer twenty to thirty minute break where you maybe take a walk, call a friend, get something to eat, or strike a few yoga poses—whatever works best for you.

I have found this idea to be tremendously helpful, particularly if I have a long day of freelance work ahead of me in which I have to write seven to eight research-heavy articles. I can feel overwhelmed about getting started, and if I'm a little tired or just not in the mood for researching, it can seem like there's no way I'll be able to get it all done.

Breaking it down into smaller chunks helps me to zero in on only the next 25-minute project, which is much more manageable. I can focus faster during that time, and before long I'm pounding out the words. When it's time to take a break, I get up and move around a bit, and I'm ready to go for that next 25-minute chunk. It's amazing how much more I get done this way than I used to working long, exhausting two- to four-hour slogs.

## Chunking Improves Productivity

There are several reasons why this technique works. First, it helps you overcome the difficulty of having to concentrate for extended periods of time. We're all about making it easier on your brain, here! It makes the task at hand seem much more doable.

Second, it gives you a time limit, so it's easier to put off distractions. You'll be done soon, and can attend to those other things at that time. That gives you permission to let them be for the moment.

Third, chunking allows you to feel a sense of accomplishment, which is incredibly motivating. After you finish the twenty-five minutes and realize you succeeded in spending that time focused on what you were doing, you can't help but feel good about it. This will motivate you to get more done, which is addictive, and helpful to you as a writer.

Many writers balk when they think about taking a break at twenty-five minutes. You may wonder if you'll actually damage your work if you're "in the flow" when the timer goes off. If things are going well, should you really stop at that point? Let's look at that question.

## Decide On Your Best Chunk Time

You may already be pretty good at focusing when you pull up your writing project. If so, is twenty-five minutes enough time to work before taking a break? Maybe for you, forty-five or fifty-five minutes would be better. That's the nice thing about this technique—it's flexible, and you can make it work for you. Set the timer for the length of time you think you can write without succumbing to distractions and go for it.

You have to be careful, though, not to work too long without a break, because you may end up feeling like you're "running on fumes," or like you've completely worn yourself out. I've come out of some writing sessions feeling like that. I'm elated over my progress, but my head is spinning, my back is sore, and I'm voraciously hungry. You've probably had similar writing sessions that left you feeling a great sense of accomplishment, but mentally and physically spent.

If you end the day this way, you run the risk of creating a dangerous scenario: the next day when it's time to write, you look at your computer and groan. Your back pain flares up, reminding you of what it felt like the day before. You feel too tired to tear into it again, so you decide to blow off writing today and get back to it tomorrow.

Be careful that you don't get so pleased with your progress on that one long day that you take two, three, or four days off and get behind. You could be setting yourself up for an unproductive outcome: abandoning the writing routine you've worked so hard to schedule and maintain. You don't want to allow yourself to break that good habit. If you do, it's going to take a lot of willpower to get back into it. The longer you wait, the harder it will be.

This is why you have to be very careful with the amount of time you set for each chunk, and be sure to give yourself adequate breaks. If you don't, you could be setting yourself up not only to get less done, but also to develop long-term health issues.

**Chunk for Health and Well-Being**

Sitting for hours working without a break is very bad for you. Studies have shown that remaining in a sitting position for more than six hours a day (and remember, that includes work, commute, television watching, etc.) is linked with a significant increase of early mortality, as well as other pesky things like heart disease, Type 2 diabetes, and cancer.

Plus you know how it feels when you sit for hours without moving: Ouch! It's one of the primary ways we exacerbate chronic knee, hip, back, and neck pain, and it also causes stiff muscles and joints.

Chunking gives you an excuse to get up, walk around, get a glass of water, look out the window (great for your tired eyes) and in general, give your brain a break. By stopping work before you get too tired, you prevent brain burnout, and leave yourself some energy for other tasks or fun activities. This also helps you leave your writing session feeling energized rather than sapped, which will be much more motivating when you go into your *next* writing session.

## Time Treasure

# Chunk It!

It's time to try chunking for yourself. Start by determining which projects (in addition to writing) you want to complete, and how long you want to concentrate during each chunk. The recommended time is twenty-five minutes. If you can focus well, feel free to increase the time. Just don't push it too far. Over one hour is usually longer than the brain can focus well without a break.

Next, make a list of all the things you want to accomplish today that require concentration, and then chunk each one. As you go about your day, make a checkmark next to your list with each chunk you complete, and mark an "X" by the project when you actually finish it.

So for example, your list might look like this:

- PowerPoint presentation for work √√
    - (you spent two chunks of time, but didn't finish it)
- Project report due to the boss √√√ X
    - (you spent three chunks of time, and finished it)
- Thirty minutes of writing time √
    - (you spent one chunk of time, but didn't finish the chapter)
- Research on potential editor for my novel √
    - (you spent one chunk of time, but didn't find an editor yet)

At the end of the day, review your progress and note how you feel about what you've accomplished. Keeping a list like this is very beneficial, as it shows in black and white just how much you were able to get done. You may have "counted" only completed projects in the past, but this method allows you to take credit for progress made on unfinished projects, as well. Seeing progress, even in small increments, motivates you to eagerly tackle your projects day after day to see how much closer you are to reaching your goals.

Try chunking for at least a week to see if it works for you. Also note how the regular practice of focusing for twenty-five minutes at a time helps make focusing easier, in general. Chunking is actually a way to practice concentration, and you are likely to get better at it as you go.

### Time Treasure

## Train the Brain to Focus Faster

In addition to chunking and making it easier on your brain to focus, it's also important to spend time training your brain to get better at focusing, in general. The goal is to get to that place where you can drop into your story within a minute or two and not come up for air until your time is up, regardless of where you are or what's going on around you. Think Luke-Skywalker-defending-against-a-laser-zapping-machine-while-blindfolded type of focus. That's where you want to be.

**Start by structuring your day.** Establishing habits helps train your brain to focus when it's time. Say you write Monday, Wednesday, and Friday from 7:00–7:30 a.m., and you tackle your most difficult project at work from 9:00–11:00 a.m. Structure allows you to settle down more quickly into a routine that works for you, and the more you follow that routine, the more quickly your brain will focus when it's time.

Next, **create pre-writing rituals.** Ritual establishes muscle memory, and the brain is like a muscle. Think about how you feel when you put on your running clothes, strap on your fitness tracker, and slip on your tennis shoes. Your body responds with a bit of adrenaline, pumping energy to your limbs before you even walk out the door. It's automatic.

You can make focusing on your writing an automatic behavior, too, by doing the same ritual every time before you start typing. You may put on your favorite sweater, for example, fix yourself a cup of green tea, go to your quiet place, and open up your computer. Or maybe you put on some music and spend five minutes breathing deeply before you start writing. Whatever you do, do it the same way every time. Your brain responds to triggers like these, and before long, whenever you start the ritual, your brain will think, "Okay, we're going to focus now," and will drop right into your story when you're ready.

**Meditation** will also help improve your ability to focus faster. Most of us have trained ourselves *not* to focus by responding to distractions all the time. Meditation can help retrain your brain out of this bad habit. You don't have to be fancy about it.

Set the timer for ten minutes, sit quietly, breathe deeply, and focus on one thing. Maybe it's an image of your favorite place, a candle flame, a spoken sound, or the flower in the corner of the room. Allow your thoughts to come and go without reacting, and keep bringing them back to your focal point.

Meditation is the perfect training for focus and concentration. The more you do it, the better you will get at it. If you try it for just a week, you'll likely notice improvements in your ability to focus on writing or anything else.

Finally, **practice delayed gratification.** If you're still finding it difficult to avoid distractions, it's time to pump up your VLPFC. Every day, find ways to resist your impulses. Start by resisting for only five minutes. If you want that donut, make yourself wait for five minutes. If you're dying to answer a text, wait for five minutes. If you feel a little chilled, give it five minutes before you put on your sweater. Practice makes perfect. The more you do it, the better you'll get at it, until you're able to focus quickly and for long periods of time without getting distracted.

As it becomes easier to sink into your story every day, broaden your application to your other projects. Ask yourself how long it takes you to focus on a task at work, for example, or on a conversation with a colleague or friend, or even on a television show. Watch yourself to see how often you are distracted, and how many times you resist those distractions.

Focus is a skill, much like skiing or playing a musical instrument or…writing! Practice, practice, practice, and you will get better.

CHAPTER 8

# KNOW YOUR TIME PERSONALITY

I'VE ALWAYS BEEN a night owl. From as far back as I can remember I preferred staying up at night to rising early in the morning. I used to sneak out of my bedroom to watch *Rockford Files* with my dad, who cared less about children's bedtimes than my mom did. She was often asleep by that time, so I could get away with it now and then.

Meanwhile, I dreaded getting up to go to school. I was always tired and groggy and half asleep, but come bedtime I couldn't get my eyes to close, so when I wasn't sneaking out to watch television with my dad, I was reading books under the covers.

No surprise, then, that when I got my first job as a writer at a big corporation, I hated having to get up early to go to work. My dream of rising when I darn well wanted to was one of the reasons I went freelance! Like most of us, when I can follow my own circadian rhythms, I sleep better, I'm happier, and I'm more productive.

You may also have an idea of what times of day work best for you for being creative and productive, but this chapter goes far beyond that. I'm going to help you define your unique time personality, which involves not only your peak energy times throughout the day and night, but how you "see" time as a whole. This part of your personality is so significant that scientists have gone so far as to say that "time perspective" is just as defining a personality characteristic as openness, conscientiousness, and introversion or extroversion.

**Personality Time Zones**

Each person's time personality is made up of four factors. Once you know where you land in each of them, you can use that knowledge to become more productive. I call them the four personality time zones:

1. Clock time vs. event time
2. Time perspective
3. Peak creative times
4. Yearly energy cycles

## PERSONALITY TIME ZONE #1: CLOCK-TIMERS VS. EVENT-TIMERS

You've heard of right-brained and left-brained people, introverts and extroverts, Type A and Type B. Now you can add "clock-timers" and "event-timers" to the list. According to recent research, we all fall into one camp or the other, and one is believed to be more conducive to creativity. Here are some basic details about the two types:

1. **Clock-timers** use the clock to organize their activities. They get up at a certain time, schedule each task between this hour and that, and in general run their daily routines by hours and minutes.

2. **Event-timers** don't pay as much attention to the clock, and organize their day by tasks to complete. They work on one project until they either finish it or reach a stopping point, and then shift to the next. They have a list of things they want to get done, and work sequentially until they either finish them all or have to stop.

So where clock-timers wake up with an alarm, event-timers wake up when they wake up. Clock-timers go home at a certain time, while event-timers will stay as long as they're enjoying the party.

We all use a little of both of these approaches in our daily lives; there's really not a lot of choice. Event-timers can't be two hours late to their three o'clock dentist appointments, for instance, or show up at the kids' band concert whenever they feel like it. Likewise, clock-timers are known to sleep in sometimes, regardless of the hour. Overall, though, we tend to favor one approach over the other.

In observing this phenomenon, researchers discovered something interesting, especially for people like writers, artists, and musicians who need to be creative: relying on the clock made people less creative, *and* less happy. Clock-timers felt less in control of their lives, as if they were run by the clock and couldn't really do what they wanted when they wanted—a feeling that tends to kill any sort of creative play. Event-timers, on the other hand, felt more in control, which is naturally associated with happiness. An event timer, for example, typically won't move on to the next task until he's done with the first one, so he feels more like he changes tasks when *he's* ready, rather than when an outside clock tells him he has to. This person is freer to pursue creative thoughts to see where they might lead.

Clock-timers also don't see as much connection between their activities. They view their day in blocks of time, each task in its scheduled time slot, with no links between them. This viewpoint leads clock-timers to experience the world as chaotic, driven more by random events than by causality.

The event-timers, on the other hand, make connections between events, because finishing one task leads to starting another. This viewpoint allows them to feel that actions create results, and to imagine they can change their lives by taking steps in the direction they want to go.

## Clock-timers vs. Event-timers

Some other interesting differences between the two types:

- **Enjoying experiences:** Because they watch the clock, clock-timers are less able to enjoy their activities, gleaning fewer good feelings from them. Event-timers are able to become totally absorbed in their experiences, and may feel more intense emotions as a result.

- **Taking control of destiny:** Event-timers attribute events to their actions, and are more likely to believe they can change things if they don't like them. Clock-timers are more likely to be resigned to their fate.

- **Remembering experiences:** Because event-timers seem to get more involved in their experiences, they often remember them more positively than clock-timers, and are better able to look back and recall their positive feelings.

- **Taking advantage of opportunities:** Clock-timers are less likely to take advantage of random opportunities, because they feel like they have to "reschedule" everything to fit in something new. Event timers are more likely to enjoy new opportunities, regardless of when they present themselves.

- **Getting in the "flow":** Clock-timers are less able to reach a meditative state while doing something like yoga, as they tend to focus on how long they have to hold a pose. They may also have more difficulty reaching the "flow" state that is so critical for creative work like writing. Event-timers are better able to sink into the experience, and to allow their minds to zone out.

Of course in today's world, being an event-timer isn't all raspberries and cream. If you have difficulty checking in with the clock, you may have trouble on the job or in your relationships because you're chronically late, or because you fail to meet deadlines. That can hurt your writing, too, if you blissfully go along creating with no thought as to when your project needs to be completed. On the whole, however, when you need to sit down and create something new on the page, watching the clock is likely to slow your progress.

No matter what type you are naturally, you may find that like most of us, you've become a slave to the clock. It's difficult to resist when you're surrounded by demands on your time. But that doesn't mean you can't approach time differently on occasion.

### Time Treasure for Clock-Timers

# Hide the Clocks!

Take a look at your week and see when you can ditch the clock, or at least fudge a little bit. It may be easiest to choose a Saturday or Sunday for this exercise, or one night a week that you generally have unscheduled time.

Allowing even just a little freedom from the shackles of measured time can help you be more productive when you sit down to write. If you need more flexibility overall, maybe it's time to propose to the boss some minor changes in your work schedule, or to ask for just one day a week when you can work different hours, or work at home.

### Time Treasure for Event-Timers

# Set More Deadlines

If you're an event-timer naturally, it will be easier for you to tune into your creativity when you sit down to write, as long as you haven't been brainwashed by our culture's reliance on the clock. If you suspect you have, see the time treasure above! If not, you may have the opposite problem—getting your projects done and out the door. That can slow down your progress toward your writing goals, especially if you're not sending your stories

> out for readers to see, either by submitting to editors and agents or publishing yourself.
>
> You may want to consider setting and keeping a few more deadlines to experience faster progress toward your goals. Think about what you hope to accomplish by the end of the year, and use a calendar to make sure you complete the steps needed to get there.

## PERSONALITY TIME ZONE #2: TIME PERSPECTIVE

In addition to being a clock-timer or an event-timer, we all have the tendency to view time in one of five different ways. That viewpoint affects everything, including how we approach finding time to write. It's important to know your viewpoint so you can use it to be as productive as possible.

Stanford University professor Philip Zimbardo is credited with discovering "time perception." He found that attitude toward time is a personality trait—much like optimism vs. pessimism, or introversion vs. extroversion—and defined five distinct types:

1. Past Positive
2. Past Negative
3. Present Hedonistic
4. Present Fatalistic
5. Future Oriented

Again, we all have some characteristics of each, but tend to favor one more than the others. If you're curious about your time perception personality, you can take Zimbardo's test online at http://www.thetimeparadox.com/zimbardo-time-perspective-inventory/.

It consists of sixty-one easy questions. Meanwhile, I've summarized the five types below. Look at each one and see which sounds most like you.

1. **Past Positive:** Overall, you prefer to focus on the past rather than the present or future, and have a mostly positive view of it. You base your decisions on past experiences, as it's difficult to imagine things being different. You're nostalgic by nature, and enjoy sharing stories of the "good old days." You have traditional values, and avoid taking risks. You find reminiscing a pleasant pastime, and like honoring family traditions and other activities that connect you to your past.

2. **Past Negative:** You also tend to think about the past a lot, but not necessarily in a good light. You may think back to traumatic experiences you had as a child, and nurse old wounds that you haven't been able to heal. You may also think about good experiences that you missed out on for one reason or another, and tend to talk about how things weren't that good in your past.

3. **Present Hedonistic:** You live in the moment, and do everything you can to make that moment enjoyable. You're all about the "now," and are likely to follow your heart over your head, even if it means having to face unpleasant consequences down the road. You indulge your senses, and like your days to be full of fun and excitement. People might describe you

as playful and impulsive—the life of the party—but may also say that sometimes you goof off too much.

4. **Present Fatalistic:** You live in the now, too, but you tend to think you can't do much about it. Your life is determined by fate, you believe, so it doesn't make much sense to you to break your back trying to change it. You may be very religious, or devoted to some other authority you believe has more power in your life than you do. You may be partial to rituals, or enjoy carrying around a good luck charm. You may also be more likely to suffer from depression, eating disorders, and addictions.

5. **Future Focused:** You are all about creating a better future for yourself and your loved ones. You tend to base your decisions on where you want to be five to ten years from now, rather than on where you were in the past. You find it easy to imagine the future, and look forward to it as being better for you than the present is. You're likely to make good choices in terms of health and finances that will set you up for long-term positive consequences. Because you are so focused on the future, however, you may find it hard to enjoy the present moment. You like to be in control, which may hurt your relationships, and you may be an anxious or stressed person much of the time.

Time Treasure

## Work with your Time Perspective

To become a more productive writer, you want to capitalize on your strengths, and then work on those areas that tend to be weaknesses for you. Now that you have an idea of what your time perspective is, you can use that knowledge to find more time to write and to become more productive in general.

### 1. Past Positive

The good news is that you tend to be a stable person overall. You have solid relationships with your family and friends, and that can help you weather the ups and downs of the writing life. You are likely to have a high self-esteem, and to feel satisfied with your life, which enables you to create with a calm heart.

You may have difficulty, though, imagining a future in which your work is published or your book selling like gangbusters, which may result in you doing less than you could to make your dreams come true. You may also find it difficult to try new things, which could hold you back from experiences that could help boost your career.

**Action Step:** What you need is to help yourself *see* the future more clearly. Create a visual collage of where you will be five years from now. You may want to use a program like Canva to add your own personal touches to your digital images. Put your book title on an image of a book, for example, or your name and class title on a schedule of writing workshops. Find other ways to help yourself imagine what your future could look like if you put the time in on your writing today.

Next, plan to do something new this year related to your writing career. Maybe you'll submit to some new publications, attend a new writer's conference, hire a book doctor, or join a writing group. Realize your tendency to hesitate when thinking about new experiences may be holding you back. Schedule the activity and put it on your calendar, and when you feel that resistance, push forward and do it anyway.

## 2. Past Negative

You share many of the same characteristics as type #1 (past-positive), but you tend to put a negative spin on things. This can make rejections and poor book sales particularly difficult for you to handle. You are likely to ruminate over these events, thinking again and again about how you were rejected or how readers just didn't understand your story to the point that you become thoroughly discouraged and depressed. This will put a stop to your progress as a writer.

**Action Step:** Realize that you tend to chew over old, negative experiences way more than most people do. Your new motto should become, "Let it go." Try writing down these negative experiences in a journal, and once the experience is recorded, promise yourself that the next time you start thinking about it, you'll find something distracting to do. Turn on your favorite music, take a drink of water, or call a friend, and do not allow yourself to talk about that negative past event!

Then, the next time you have one of these negative experiences, take an opposite, positive action. Don't pay attention to how you feel—just do it. Have a list of agents or editors, for example, so that when one rejects you, you can send the story back out to the next one, no thinking required. When one writing time doesn't work for you, have an alternate time "in the wings" so you can try again the next day. Always have a "do this next" activity planned so you don't get caught up in negative thinking. Remember that action begets emotion—you need to *do* something positive before you will feel more positive.

### 3. Present Hedonistic

You are the person who writes with joy and abandon, and gets just as big a kick out of the process as the rewards. You enjoy writing for writing's sake, and are likely to have lots of work that you will never publish, and that's just fine with you.

Where you may struggle is in taking that next step in your career. You may want to publish a novel, for example, but find that it keeps eluding you because you don't have a real career plan. You may find it difficult to finish a novel, because it gets tough in the middle, so you just abandon it and start something new. Hey, that's more fun!

**Action Step:** Realize that just because a story starts to get difficult doesn't mean it's no longer worth pursuing. Practice writing through the hard parts, and make a commitment to finish at least one project a year. If you're a poet or short story writer, complete at least three to five projects a year. Make "finishing" just as high a priority as having fun with your writing.

Next, focus on creating a step-by-step plan for your writing career. If you want to be earning money from your stories in five years, for example, get out a calendar and decide where you need to be by the end of each year to make that happen. Then break it down further so you can set monthly deadlines for yourself. Most importantly, create rewards for your progress. Present Hedonistic people like feeling good, so try to reward yourself for small tasks that you complete to motivate yourself to keep going.

### 4. Present Fatalistic

You may be struggling in your writing career because you feel like whatever you do makes no difference. You may blame your failures on the market, agents and editors, publishers, eBooks, or what have you. You may see the publishing world as being unfair, and suffer from depression.

The problem is that you feel you have no power in your life.

**Action Step:** It's going to be difficult for you to progress as a writer if you don't try to change your thinking just a little bit. The most important thing is to show yourself that you *can* make a difference in your life, at least as far as your writing goes.

There are a lot of things that are, indeed, out of your control. Whether a publisher gives you a contract, whether other people buy your books, or whether your writing wins an award is mostly out of your hands. That means you must find meaning in the act of writing itself.

Focus on how writing benefits your life. Leave all the rest of it—publishing, sales, recognition—out of the picture, and focus on yourself as an artist. You are called to write. Think about how that gives your life meaning, and devote yourself to the practice. Then, make it your goal to submit your writing more often. Even though it probably won't make any difference, submit anyway. You may be surprised at the eventual outcome.

### 5. Future Focused

The good news is that you are tailor-made for the long haul of the writing business. You are focused on the future, and have no problem toiling away for years working toward your eventual goals. You work hard on your writing, and you have a very clear idea of where you're going that helps you set goals and reach them.

You also tend to have high energy, and take good care of your health so that you will enjoy many years of productive writing. Your problem is that you work too hard and worry too much, which can set you up for a hard crash or burnout. You can exhaust yourself with all that effort, to the point that you collapse and struggle to get going again.

**Action Step:** Make it a point to take time off more frequently than you think you should. Plan a yearly long vacation, at least three shorter (four-day) vacations, and weekly days when you enjoy leisure time activities that restore you.

> Watch for signs of burnout, such as fatigue and insomnia, weight loss or gain, skin breakouts, headaches, muscle aches and pains, and a growing apathy toward your work. Remind yourself that it's not healthy in the long run to ignore your close relationships, or to make life all work and no play. Find ways to tap into your inner child so that you keep your creativity alive.

## PERSONALITY TIME ZONE #3: PEAK CREATIVE TIMES

The third factor in your unique time personality is your own energy ebb and flow. You naturally have times when you're ready to go, and other times when you'd prefer to take a nap. These highs and lows see-saw back and forth throughout the day and night. Learning to capitalize on your high-energy times can naturally increase productivity.

Unfortunately, writers often ignore their energy peaks and valleys, and write whenever they have a spare minute, rather than when energy is at its peak. Sometimes that can't be helped, but it's always best to create when you have the most energy to do so.

The key is to pinpoint your high-energy times, and schedule your most taxing projects, like writing, during those times. Most people feel their highest level of energy first thing in the morning, or sometime before noon. But others experience a second wind later in the day, or do their best work late at night.

Time Treasure

## Find Your Peak Creative Times

- **Keep an "energy diary" for two weeks.** Use your smartphone, computer, or a small notebook to keep track of those times when you feel really tired, and when you feel most awake and alert. Include weekend days.

- Once you have two weeks of data, analyze it to **pinpoint the best and worst times** for getting your work done.

- **Rearrange your schedule** to do the most difficult projects during high-energy times, and the easiest at low-energy times. You may have to compromise a little in some cases, but draw it up as closely as you can.

- **Schedule recovery time.** Most writers feel they can't take more than five minutes for a break, but that's actually counterproductive. Either practice the chunking technique we talked about earlier, or at the very least, keep in mind that taking regular breaks improves focus and sustains your energy. Schedule a ten-minute break each hour, and a half-hour break every four hours. In addition, give yourself an hour after work to do something non-work related (like exercising or spending quality time with family). These break times will restore your body, mind, and creativity.

- **Keep tweaking your schedule.** You'll probably have to

> do some tweaking before you land on a schedule that works best. Re-evaluate it every couple of weeks to determine your energy flow, and change it up as needed.

## PERSONALITY TIME ZONE #4: YEARLY ENERGY CYCLES

Similar to daily peaks and valleys, we have yearly ups and downs that influence productivity. When winter comes around, for example, I notice a decrease in my energy level and feel the need to hibernate a bit. But it's also the time I tend to get a lot of my writing done. The cold air and the cloudy days inspire a quiet, concentrated mood in me. As the weather warms up, I love being outside, and resent having to work indoors when I could be jogging or hiking in the sunshine.

One of the things I hope you take from this book is the ability to be flexible with your time (and energy) management. A schedule that works in January may not work in July. Writer's workshops tend to rev up in the summertime, for example, and book sales are usually highest then, too. You need to take advantage of these times to give your work the best chance to succeed, but you want to keep writing, too. That means you often have to juggle the different parts of your schedule depending on the time of year.

It takes commitment to track your personal cycles over a twelve-month period, but I encourage you to start doing it now. Notice when you tend to naturally gravitate toward writing, and when you are more likely to want to get out, do some research or interviews, attend workshops, take classes, or simply get away from the computer for a while.

*Time Treasure*

## Discover Your Yearly Energy Cycles

Using any type of calendar (printed, digital, whatever), choose one day a week—Sunday, for example—and record your overall creative energy for the previous week. Write down the days and times when you felt motivated and inspired to work on your writing projects, and what specific projects you were working on. Then write down the days when you felt tired and had to force yourself to create, and what projects you were working on then. Note how much you enjoyed actually writing, as opposed to other writing-related activities like building your website or attending conferences.

After a year of doing this, you will start to see a number of things:

- when your creative energy cycles wax and wane,
- what type of writing you most enjoy and when,
- what type of writing-related projects are most fatiguing for you, or are more difficult for you to accomplish,
- which seasons are most high-energy for you, and which are low,
- which months are the most productive,
- and when you need extra motivation to keep going.

> As you grow more familiar with your own "quirks" when it comes to all these things, you'll be better able to plan your next year's schedule more effectively.

**Put it All Together**

Now that you've determined your unique time personality in each of the four time zones, write the results below:

1. Clock-timer or event-timer? _____

2. Time perspective (past-positive, future-focused, etc.) _____
   _____

3. Peak energy times (write down at least three that occur each day, such as between 9 and 10 a.m.)

   a. _____
   b. _____
   c. _____

4. Yearly energy cycle (write down three months in the year when you seem to have the most energy for writing itself—if you don't have this information yet, make your best guess until you do)

   a. _____
   b. _____
   c. _____

You've just learned a ton about yourself and your personal approach to time. Put this list somewhere you can see it everyday, and let it remind you of what you need to do to find *your* best times to write. Then begin to work with (rather than against) your own personality to become a less stressed and more productive writer.

CHAPTER 9

# SAY "NO"

I KNEW A MAN in my community who was one of the most creative and hard-working people you could ever meet. A friendly, casual guy, he spent his days teaching music to high school students, which also required him to attend many related sporting events, concerts, contests, and field trips on weekends and evenings. In between, he lent his talents as a performer to local music groups, while maintaining an open-door policy to anyone who needed him.

I often marveled at how he seemed to handle it all, and then found out one day that he had been appointed to a leadership position in his church that would require even more of his time and devotion. He never let on that any of it was taxing, but I started to worry that he was trying to do too much. Still, I, along with the rest of the community, was shocked when at a young age years before retirement, he suddenly passed away.

The cause of death was some sort of heart condition, and I certainly can't say if his hectic schedule aggravated it, but I do know that if we want to stay healthy and productive, we can't be all things to all people. We have to respect our limits.

The problem is that sticking to what we know is good for us often entails doing something that can be very difficult: saying "no" to other people. We all want to help others, avoid conflict, and be nice, so we sometimes agree to do things that aren't in our best interests and end up stealing our creative time away.

Most writers would agree that they tend to give in more often than they should, and then they end up resenting the lost writing time. Yet it can be so difficult to say this one word when you need to. This chapter will show you how to be more decisive about donating time to others, so you preserve more time for your writing…and your sanity.

**Address the Conflict Within**

Here's how three different writers lost their writing time because of the difficulty of saying "no."

Betsy was an aspiring writer who for years had dreamed of penning her own stories and holding her published books in her hands. When her last child left for college, she made a commitment to write for an hour every morning between eight and nine o'clock. She was nearly halfway through her first novel-length manuscript when her older daughter, Sarah, moved back to town.

Betsy was thrilled. She had really missed Sarah and looked forward to seeing her more often. Even more exciting was being able to see her three-year-old grandson, Jacob. About two weeks after their reunion, Sarah got a job as a nurse. She immediately asked her mother if she'd mind babysitting. Betsy jumped at the chance, but after watching Jacob for over ten hours a day five days a week, she realized she wasn't getting any writing done. She tried to change her writing time to the night hours after Jacob went home, but by that time, she was worn out.

Betsy hung in there for six weeks, but her fatigue worsened, while her novel sat on her desk untouched. She started to resent the time she was spending babysitting, and mourned her lack of creative writing time. Her husband told her to speak to their daughter. Surely Sarah could find childcare at least a couple times a week, he said. But Betsy couldn't imagine it. She could never tell her daughter that she needed more time for herself, and to write a novel, of all things. She just couldn't appear to be that "selfish."

Mike, meanwhile, also an aspiring writer, worked a corporate job. He wanted to write after work, before going home to his family, but his friends always asked him to go for a drink during that time. Mike liked the feeling of belonging to the group, and didn't know how to tell his friends that he couldn't go with them. Yet he had no other time in his schedule for writing. He continued to go with his friends, but felt worse about it every day.

Laura, a newly published author who cooked dinner for her family every night, was finding it difficult to keep up with both her writing and her new marketing tasks. She finally told her husband that she would be spending Monday and Wednesday evenings writing, and that he and the boys would have to fend for themselves. It went okay for a couple weeks, until the boys got tired of pizza and hot dogs and started begging Laura to resume cooking her delicious meals. Instead of staying true to herself, Laura caved, and returned to being home chef.

"It was nice to feel appreciated," she told her friends.

Betsy, Mike, and Laura all believe their situations are temporary, but this is magical thinking. Chances are they will all be in similar predicaments five or even ten years down the road unless they change their priorities and allow their writing to come first.

## Get Over the Fear

We are social creatures. We like to feel we belong to the group, and when we go against the tide, we can end up alone. That's a scary feeling—one that often compels us to say "yes" despite our better judgment.

There's also the worry that saying "no" will make others think negatively about us. The last thing Betsy wants, for example, is for her daughter to think she doesn't want to spend time with her grandson, or that she doesn't adore them both.

Yet psychologists say this concern is generally overblown in our minds. Most people won't take "no" as seriously as we think they will. In fact, we often sell others short in this way. Sarah, for example, may feel hurt when she discovers that her mother was halfway through her novel and gave it up to babysit Jacob, all because she thought her daughter wouldn't understand. Laura's family, too, may feel badly when they learn she feels obligated to cook for them when she has her own dreams she's neglecting.

It can also be frightening to say "no" because of how we were raised. Most children were taught to be nice, make people happy, and help out, which can make saying "no" doubly difficult as adults. It feels like we're going against everything we've ever been taught.

Perhaps the biggest fear is that of conflict. Some people just don't want to hear the word "no." Say the word and you can expect an argument, or at least a conflict of some sort. It may seem easier to say "yes" just to keep the peace.

With all these fears, it's no wonder it can be difficult to say "no." What you must realize is the very real cost of failing to do so.

## Understand the Creative Cost

It's difficult for others to understand the nature of writing and what it takes in terms of time and energy, especially if they're not writers themselves. "It's only an afternoon," they may say, but you have to measure the creative cost as well as the time cost.

Remember, you're not a machine. You have only so many hours in the day that are high energy. You have to figure how much less you will create if you agree to a request, how much momentum you will lose on your project, and how much time will it take you to build that momentum up again.

If you rearranged your schedule to include writing time, never forget or discount the importance of that commitment and what you had to do to make it work. Maybe you sacrificed another activity or spent weeks mapping out a new workable schedule. Value the effort and the voice inside you that reminds you how important writing is to you and your personal evolution.

Overall productivity rests on how well you stick with your schedule. Yes, things are bound to happen and you need to stay flexible, but if you are making it worse by saying "yes" when you should be saying "no," your writing time will suffer.

## Time is Money

Imagine for a moment that time is money. If Betsy's daughter asked her for three hundred dollars a week instead of five days' worth of babysitting, Betsy probably wouldn't feel guilty or wrong about setting limits and requiring her daughter to support herself.

If Mike's friends asked him to pay for all the drinks every day after work, he would probably have no trouble turning them down. If Laura's children asked her to give them ten dollars every night rather than fix dinner, she'd probably put the brakes on that idea right quick.

When people ask us for money, it's easier to weigh the request logically in terms of what we have available to give. Yet we often have difficulty seeing time in the same way. We imagine it's more plentiful, even when time is the most important thing we must invest if we want to achieve our creative goals.

---

### Time Treasure

## Say "No" and Feel Good About It

Here are some ways to say "no" that minimize guilt, while reducing the chance that the other person will take it negatively. Don't lose sight of the fact that you need to stay true to yourself regardless of how others react.

**1. Say, "Let me think about it."**
This is an extremely effective technique I use all the time. It gives you the space to truly evaluate the request, determine the creative cost, and come up with an answer.

After a day or two has passed, you can honestly say, "I thought about it, and unfortunately I've just got too much on my plate right now." Most people will understand that or a similar type of answer. What's important is that you gain the time and space you need to make your best decision. The other person is also likely to respect that it took time to make this important decision and that you just didn't brush him or her off.

Another benefit to this approach is that people often forget to get back to you! By simply asking for some time, you avoided any conflict in the moment, and later discovered that the request may not have been all that important to the person who made it.

### 2. Truly evaluate the creative cost.

To avoid feeling guilty, remind yourself that any time spent on another project requires you to not only sacrifice that time, but to inconvenience yourself by having to shift around your entire schedule. That can sap your energy and often your motivation. Even if you take time away only from your leisure activities, that's downtime you needed to recharge your mental batteries and maintain your creativity.

There is *always* a price to pay, so before you say "yes," evaluate the true cost!

### 3. Resist being a people pleaser.

If you frequently have trouble saying no, you may be a people pleaser. This intense need to please others is often rooted in fears of failure and rejection. To reduce this tendency, think about the people you admire in life—your heroes. Most likely you admire them not because they're "nice" or because they always say "yes," but because they strive to reach their goals and dreams, show tenacity and focus, and stay true to their purpose.

As a creative person, you have a sense of what you want to do and who you want to become. These visions rarely involve pleasing everyone. When you need to say "no," take comfort in the fact that you're staying true to your creative purpose and becoming more like your heroes every day.

### 4. Give simple answers.

Don't torture yourself when trying to say "no." Instead, say as little as possible. Others will likely feel disappointed regardless of what you say or how you say it, so don't drag it out. Besides, you don't owe anyone an explanation. Saying, "I'm sorry, I've got a prior engagement," is enough. "It sounds like a great project, but I'm just swamped right now." Or, "I'd love to participate, but now just isn't a good time."

If the other person presses you, simply repeat your answer. If that's not enough, just keep repeating. Eventually the message will get through. This saves you from having to come up with any big long explanation that will likely get you into more conflict.

### 5. Learn to say, "I don't."

Researchers reported in a 2012 study that saying "I don't" is more effective when trying to resist a request than saying "I can't." Students who wanted to eat healthier diets were presented with a piece of chocolate cake. Those who said, "I don't eat chocolate cake," felt more empowered and were better able to resist than those who said, "I can't eat chocolate cake."

Saying "I don't do X" signals a fixed attitude toward your commitments. "I can't," on the other hand, is less empowering and more likely to result in caving into temptation.

Rather than think, "I can't miss my writing time," say to yourself, "I don't miss my writing time." This will give you the strength to say "no."

### 6. Think of "no" as "yes."
Whenever you say "no" to someone, don't focus on that "no." Instead, focus on the "yes" you're actually saying to yourself.

If you must turn down a friend's request to help him/her move because you had that time set aside to finish your novel, focusing on the time you're saving to go after your dreams will make it easier to say, "I'm sorry, I have a prior commitment."

### 7. Develop the skill of saying, "No."
Like all creative endeavors, saying "no" requires skill. You have to educate yourself, practice, get feedback, and improve.

Start by practicing on simple requests. When a clerk asks if you want to upsize your drink, for example, you could say, "I can't drink that much," or "That's okay." Sensing your uncertainty, the clerk may press you by saying, "But it's only fifty cents more."

You can often stop this uncomfortable situation with a decisive "no." Say it firmly, in full voice, and make eye contact. It's a great way to practice with no downside!

If you keep looking for opportunities like this, you'll see that it's not a big deal to say "no" when you truly mean it. You may even start to have fun as you get better at it. Over time, your guilty feelings will naturally evaporate.

### 8. Build your confidence.

I know it's difficult to imagine until you've done it a few times, but the more you say "no," the more devoted you will become to your writing. This is the other side of the coin.

By honoring your own commitments, you increase self-confidence and motivation. You teach yourself that your creative work is important, and by following through with your actions, you become stronger. Your whole physical and mental being aligns with your new purpose, creating a wealth of support and encouragement.

All that, from one little word. It's *that* powerful.

CHAPTER 10

# TRICK YOURSELF INTO GETTING STARTED

I F YOU'VE SEEN the animated blockbuster, "Happy Feet," you may remember a scene where Ramon, an Adélie penguin played by Robin Williams, must jump off a very high cliff. All of his friends charge the cliff and leap off at once, but Ramon stops himself at the last moment, too frightened to take the plunge.

Teetering on the edge, he tells himself that he can do this—he just needs to trick himself. He points to something behind him. *Look at that!* he says, and turns around to look. In the midst of the turn, he naturally falls over the cliff after his friends, hollering all the way.

I love this scene because it demonstrates what I often have to do to get myself to write: I have to trick myself. The good news is, it works. Just like Ramon gets himself off that cliff, you can get yourself to work, increase your productivity, and get more done in a day than you thought possible—even when you don't feel like it—by using this fun little technique.

### Trick the Inner Child into Doing What You Want

Growing up, I spent quite a bit of time looking after my two brothers, who were seven and eleven years younger than me. In addition to babysitting at various times, I often fixed them dinner and helped them get ready for bed.

I don't care how old you are, it's tough to get kids to go to bed. To avoid the typical arguments, I created a way to "trick" my brothers into believing bedtime was an exciting, fun experience. I'd start by reading them a story or two, and then I'd lift each one into my arms, swing him back and forth three times (one, two, three!) and then half-toss, half plop him down in his bed. Both boys thought this was a total blast, and pretty soon, when Mom said it was time for bed, they'd charge up the stairs giggling the whole way.

Adults often act like children when it's time to get to work. "Aw, do I have to? I don't feel like it. I'm really tired. Can't I just watch TV?" The inner child fights to get his or her way, and it can be a tough battle at times.

Mind you, listening to that little "tyke" within isn't always a bad thing—we need to tap into our childlike sense of wonder when we're daydreaming, and enjoy that playfulness when crafting a story. But we also have to be aware of the child-like desire to avoid work at all costs and be ready to trick ourselves when we need to get something done.

## Overcome the Inner Child's Tendency to Procrastinate

Writing is often difficult, and no matter how much you enjoy it, it can still feel like hard work. That means your inner child will beg, tease, and whine in the hopes you'll avoid writing and relax instead. If you don't maintain control, you'll waste the thirty minutes you planned to write.

One day of this procrastination isn't going to kill your writing dreams. The problem is that one day often turns into two, and then more and more until you simply aren't getting any writing done. Of course, we all procrastinate from time to time, but beware, because this tendency quickly sabotages your productivity. What's more, researchers reported in 2016 that those who procrastinated suffered higher levels of stress; more depression, anxiety, and fatigue; and reduced satisfaction across many areas in life, especially in work and income.

That's why it's better to trick yourself into doing the writing you planned to do.

---

**Time Treasure**

## The 5-Minute Trick

The next time you hear your inner child whining about being too tired or restless to write, tell him that you'll write for just five minutes, and then crash in the easy chair. Five minutes is all you need to manage. Keep talking to yourself. Don't change clothes. Don't open your email. Just go to your desk, turn on your computer, and sit down. Open your file and start writing. Five minutes. That's all.

Most of the time, your love of writing will take over and you won't want to stop after the five minutes is up. You'll happily complete your thirty minutes, and you'll feel super proud of yourself, because you'll be one step closer to achieving your writing goals—all good outcomes simply because you decided to trick yourself.

It's a simple technique, but it works really well. Let's look at why that is.

## Getting Past the Four Stoppers

The hardest part of *any* task is just getting started. You have to get past any initial resistance to doing whatever job you have in front of you. That means bypassing the four "stoppers:"

1. Perceived Difficulty
2. Perceived Importance
3. Fear
4. Expectations

One, you perceive the project ahead as being difficult. Writing a story, for example, isn't usually an "easy" thing to do. It requires effort, and by default, you'd usually rather relax than work, particularly after a long day, or when you didn't get enough sleep the night before.

Two, you perceive the project as being important. The more important the project is, the more intimidating it is. You hesitate to start because you don't feel up to the task. You should be more alert to do it right, you think, and fear starting when you feel tired and irritable.

This brings us to stopper number three: fear. You fear you won't be able to complete the task well, so you avoid it. This is often true when it's time to write. It's why you may wait until you feel "inspired" to do so, which slows progress.

Wrapped up in that fear are your high expectations—stopper number four. You want the report to wow the boss so you can ask for a raise or you want your short story to place in an upcoming contest. Expectations build the project up in your mind, making you even more fearful, intimidated, and overwhelmed by the perceived difficulty ahead.

It's no wonder it's hard to get started! But of course you can't keep putting things off. You must learn to trick yourself into leaping off that cliff.

> **Time Treasure**
>
> ## Tricks for Getting Started
>
> Although the five-minute trick is my favorite for getting past the four stoppers, there are other options that may work even better for you.
>
> **1. Set deadlines.**
> If the boss expects your report on a certain date, that encourages you to get started on it. You have no similar supervisor for your creative work, though. That means you have to set up your own deadlines, and stick to them.
>
> If you want to write a novel this year, map it out on your calendar, allowing a week per chapter or whatever works for your process. The particular timeframe doesn't really matter in the beginning—just getting something down on a calendar will help you overcome procrastination. Be sure to hang it somewhere you can see it on a daily basis.

## 2. Make it fun.

I typically spend the first five minutes of my writing time reading. It's a lot easier to read a book than face a blank page. By the time the five minutes are up, I'm in the writing "mood" and ready to go.

Reading may work for you, too, or you could listen to music, fix a cup of tea, or get yourself something tasty to munch on. Indulge yourself for a few minutes so the start of the whole process seems pleasurable. This will help overcome any resistance you may feel.

## 3. Make it a habit.

Setting and sticking with a certain writing time for even just a week will establish a habit. That means if you *don't* write during that time it will feel strange. The human brain and body are made to adopt new habits. If I eat a donut two mornings in a row, for example, I'll likely find myself eating a donut every morning from then on if I'm not careful!

Habits are easier to make than break, so use this tendency to your advantage. Stick to your schedule for a week, and it will become harder for your inner child to lure you away.

## 4. Put off something else.

You can trick yourself into getting started on an important task by allowing yourself to procrastinate on another one. Imagine you have a number of things on your to-do list. If your resistance is high and your inner child is whining, give in a little.

Decide that if you get your writing done, you'll put off something else on the list—getting the oil changed, for example, or doing the laundry.

It's amazing how good it can feel to allow yourself to procrastinate on *something*. Give yourself that reward to help you get started on the thing that really matters—your writing.

### 5. Pretend it's just for practice.

On super important projects, it's easy to psyche yourself out worrying you won't be able to do a good enough job. Instead, trick yourself by pretending you're simply practicing. Tell yourself this isn't the version you're going to send out. Instead, you're just practicing how you *might* do it. There's no risk, as no one is going to see this version. This is just for play, for practice, and for fun. This sort of thinking helps you plow past the four stoppers.

### 6. Commit to just one percent.

Ask yourself what you can do right now to move your project forward by just one percent. Everyone can accomplish that much. If your chapters are usually 4,000 words, one percent of that is only forty words. Even your inner child couldn't object to writing forty words.

This trick works with all kinds of projects. If you need to clean the house, maybe one percent of that is cleaning the sink—only the sink—in the bathroom. If you need to catch up on emails, maybe one percent is around three emails. Calculate your one percent and go for it. Once you get started, you'll likely finish way more than that.

### 7. Celebrate.
The brain responds to rewards. Getting a raise at work motivates you to work a little harder. Likewise, getting one story published will motivate you to write another.

Unfortunately, creative people don't often receive outside rewards. Let's face it: a month spent meeting all your writing goals won't be rewarded with a monetary bonus or two tickets to the game. That means if you don't reward yourself, there will be no rewards (outside of the satisfaction for the work you've completed).

The key to staying productive is to instill within yourself good feelings about getting your stuff done. When you meet all your writing goals, reward yourself perhaps with a weekend away, an evening out with friends, a treasured purchase, or a day off work. That way, you'll associate completing your goals with good, positive feelings. Those feelings, in turn, will make it easier to get started on the next project.

## Combine Your Present and Future Selves

Some creative people really struggle with procrastination, and may need more help getting started than the previous tips provide. If that's you, consider this: Researchers have discovered that some of us are more prone to procrastination because we have difficulty imagining our future selves.

It turns out that people who put things off for tomorrow tend to separate their present selves from their future selves more definitively, seeing them as two separate people rather than two versions of the same person. They also find it hard to relate to that future self, and feel little concern that he or she will have to manage unfinished projects down the road.

Procrastination has been called "short-term mood repair," as it helps you feel better *now*. The consequences of that procrastination are borne by your future self. It's that person who must deal with an incomplete story, not your present self who gets to enjoy goofing off.

People who feel disconnected from their future selves also use different parts of their brains when thinking of that future person. In a 2009 study, researchers found that certain areas of the brain activated differently for some people when thinking of their present selves then when thinking of their future selves. For these folks, the brain acted like it was imagining a stranger when imagining the future self.

Think about this when examining your own tendency to procrastinate. If you find it difficult to imagine yourself a year or even a month down the road, that may be contributing to your difficulty in getting started on your writing projects.

---

### Time Treasure

## Envision Your Future Self

Use your imaginative skills to think about how it will feel to be that future self who has failed to get her writing done a month from now, or a year from now. When your inner child wants you

> to goof off, take five minutes to imagine how your future self will feel about that. Draw or write about that person. Ask yourself if that's who you want to be, or if you'd rather be the one who feels proud for sticking to her guns and reaching her goals.
>
> When you resist getting started on your writing, picture that future you standing in front of you. Imagine what she would tell you to do right now, and then do it.

### Focus on Getting Started

You may come up with even more ways to trick yourself into getting started on your writing projects. Remember that getting started is ninety percent of the battle. Once you get going, you'll be fine. It's getting over the initial hurdle that is the most difficult, so rather than becoming fixated on what you have to accomplish, focus only on finding a way to begin.

CHAPTER 11

# TAKE A BREAK

When I first moved from Colorado to Idaho, before I started writing seriously, I took a job as an activities director for the Alzheimer's unit at a local nursing home. I was in charge of entertainment for a group of about twenty seniors, all diagnosed with Alzheimer's disease, who were full-time residents at the facility.

I was hired mostly because I play piano and accordion, and both were a hit with this group of folks. I played in the main gathering room for about an hour each day surrounded by elderly people clapping, singing, sitting quietly, or pacing back and forth. I also coordinated exercise classes, shopping trips to the local department store, and field trips around town to see the sights and of course, to get some ice cream.

I had a lot of unique experiences while working there, and many were memorable, but the one lesson I learned that I've never forgotten was this: It's critical to take time off.

My boss's boss, the guy who ran the facility, was a slim man with brown hair and glasses. He always wore a tie to work, and had an easy energy and happy personality. He ran a few meetings each year that all employees were required to attend, and at one of these he spoke about the issue of vacation.

I've had a lot of jobs over the years, and one thing I know is that bosses, in general, aren't super ecstatic when employees take time off. This man was different. He stood up in front of us all—nurses, cooks, coordinators, receptionists, maintenance people, and more—and proceeded to encourage everyone to use their vacation days, preferably two weeks at a time.

"You people are caregivers," he explained, "and this is a tough gig. I want you to get away and take some time to relax and restore yourselves. A week isn't sufficient. It helps you to recover somewhat, but it's not long enough to really regenerate your body and mind. I want you to come back refreshed and ready to work, so please, don't leave those vacation days unused. You all need real time off and I want you to take it."

I remember listening in total shock, my mouth half open. The big boss was encouraging people to take their vacations, two weeks at a time. I felt I had fallen into an alternate reality.

That was a long time ago, and since then, I've never again heard anyone in charge of any company or business encourage workers to take time off. Turns out that the man who ran the nursing home was smarter than all the rest. He got it, and now I'd like you to get it, too.

## Make Time Off a Priority

According to "Project Time Off," forty percent of American workers leave vacation time unused. A more recent Harris Interactive survey found that American employees use only about half of their paid time off. Worse, nearly two-thirds work while they're on vacation.

The U.S. Travel Association says that a third of us feel we can't afford it, forty percent of us fear coming back to a mountain of work, and thirty-five percent of us fear leaving our work in someone else's hands. Seventeen percent worry about losing their jobs.

Unfortunately, all this work isn't making us more productive. After a certain point (about fifty hours), productivity takes a nosedive, and those extra hours don't do anything but wear you out. In a 2015 study, for instance, scientists discovered that managers couldn't tell the difference between employees that actually worked eighty hours a week and those that just pretended to.

Meanwhile, a lifetime of long hours at work is linked to increased risk of heart disease, depression, and dementia. What writers really need to remember, though, is that overwork kills creativity. Time off, on the other hand, restores creative thinking, and recharges your abilities to come up with new ideas.

## Use Your Vacation Time

That boss I had at the nursing home made it plain that employees owed it not only to themselves, but to their patients, to take significant time off. I heard something similar a few years later when I was working my first job as a creative writer for a corporation.

The company paid for us to attend a seminar on creativity, and I remember vividly the speaker telling us that it was our responsibility to do what we had to do to maintain our creative abilities.

"Your company hired you for your creative skills," she told us. "That's what they're paying you for. So if you need some time off to restore yourself, you're obligated take it, not only for your own well being and progress, but for the company's as well."

You are the creative individual. You are the one who understands how your brain works, and what you need to do your job well. If you overwork yourself to the point of not being able to come up with new ideas, that's your fault, not anyone else's.

Take ownership over what you're doing, whether it's for money or for artistic fulfillment. Do what you need to do to reach your full potential.

---

### Time Treasure

## Work More Vacation Time into Your Annual Schedule

It's easy to talk about creating more downtime for yourself, and often difficult to actually make it happen. Here are a few tips to help you get started.

**1. Establish a vacation fund.**
Decide how much you need for a two-week vacation (two weeks is the gold standard to truly refresh your body and mind), and then figure out how much you need to save per week. Planning your vacation ahead of time can help motivate you to put that money aside. Saving money can also make your vacation plans seem more doable, adding to the momentum.

**2. Work a vacation into your yearly plan.**
If you don't add it to your calendar, it can be easy to forego your vacation. I usually make reservations for my next year's vacation at the end of the current year's stay, so that I'm "locked in," the dates set aside and scheduled with hotel reservations and all.

The one year I failed to do that, I didn't take the vacation, and I felt burned out and overwhelmed as a result.

Decide when you're going. Consider the ebb and flow of your work, and plan your vacation during non-peak times to increase your odds that everything will go smoothly. Then block it out on your calendar. You don't even have to know where you're going, just name the dates and then imagine it's written in stone.

### 3. Work hard ahead of time.

Getting ready for vacation often takes a lot of work. You may have to double up on assignments so that everything is taken care of while you're gone. It can get tough, but it's so worth it. When you're driving along the beach with the windows down or heading out for a new hike through a national park, you'll be grateful for the extra time you put into preparing for those moments.

### 4. Set boundaries.

Nothing ruins your away time more than feeling like you "have" to respond to a boss or a client via email or phone. Set clear boundaries while you're away. The second you answer an email, you destroy your chances of having a work-free vacation. Set up an automatic responder. Let people know that you're away, and refer them to a colleague if their request can't wait.

You may feel too nervous to do this initially, but if you communicate clearly beforehand, letting your clients or boss know what's up, you'll be surprised at how easy it is. You deserve to take real time off—without working while you're gone.

### 5. Give yourself some time when you get back.

Here's a tip—if you're going to be back on a Tuesday, tell your clients or your boss that you'll be back in the office Thursday. This isn't to be sneaky, but to give yourself the time you'll need to catch up.

Managing their workload upon returning from vacation was one of the main reasons people gave for not going on vacation in the first place. Make it easier on yourself. Take at least a day (or two) to catch up on emails, get organized, unpack, and settle back into your routine before you have to deal with new work requests.

### 6. Plan more frequent, short breaks.

By itself, one three-day weekend a year isn't going to give you the same benefits as a full two weeks. Shorter breaks throughout the year, though, can help you cope with a heavy workload and keep your creative gears turning smoothly.

In addition to your yearly vacation, schedule at least four of these shorter breaks throughout the year. Take advantage of national holidays and other common slow times and give yourself a long weekend to do something besides work. Don't fool yourself into thinking you can't afford to do it. The truth is that you can't afford not to. Time off boosts productivity, and you need it to be as efficient as you can be.

### 7. Leave in the middle of the week.

I have found that when I leave on a Wednesday or Thursday, I have the first few days in the week to make sure all my clients are good to go, and I'm more likely to leave without projects hanging over my head. Returning mid-week also makes it seem to my clients as if I haven't been gone as long—a bonus. Mid-week airline flights can be a lot less expensive than weekend ones too.

### 8. Get over the guilt.

Conscientious employees may feel guilty about leaving work. Unfortunately, that often leads to checking emails, making calls, and researching stuff online while the beach beckons out the window.

If you tend to feel guilty about enjoying some real time off, remember: Time off is critical to your productivity, and in essence, your ability to succeed at your job. Investing in some time off is investing in your future.

### 9. Work breaks into your everyday routine.

As you work toward your writing goals, you may frequently spend your weekends at the computer, or your evenings editing and researching agents and editors. As you try to get ahead with your writing while working a day job at the same time, you may fall into the trap of seeing every spare moment as a moment to do creative work.

Remember that overwork kills creativity. Schedule in some downtime on a weekly basis. Maybe one day a week you don't touch your computer or smartphone. Maybe you schedule in an hour each day to just walk and daydream. Every weekend take at least two hours to enjoy an activity with your family.

Pencil it in. If you don't, it's less likely to happen, which will hurt your work in the long run.

### 10. Nap.

A short nap of twenty to thirty minutes can boost your mood, improve performance and alertness, and even increase creativity. In 2008, researchers reported that naps were more effective for improving verbal memory, motor skills, and perceptual learning than caffeine was. They later found that an hour's nap dramatically boosted and restored brainpower.

Naps are also great for your health overall, as they tend to lower your blood pressure and protect your heart. Shoot for no more than thirty minutes. If you really need more time you can take it—just realize it will take you longer to fully wake up again.

## Final Note: Take a Writing Retreat

I have one more strong suggestion for increasing your creative productivity: take a writing retreat, preferably, once a year. Even if you're not working full time, in addition to pursuing your writing and creative goals, you likely have other things in your life that take up a lot of your concentration. A writing retreat allows you to focus exclusively on your craft, which can be incredibly powerful for you, and will likely increase your productivity and motivation to write when you return.

A retreat, particularly if it includes a workshop, can definitely stretch you—which is gold for creativity. You may be required to show your writing to others, or at least to create something while you're there, which can give you that added pressure to really produce. Pushing your personal boundaries and getting out of your comfort zone will help you get more done and discover new ways to tap into your own creative powers.

A retreat can also send a powerful signal to the brain that says, "This is important." If you've been neglecting your writing lately, a retreat can help you get back on track. If you have a project that's been languishing, it can help you breathe new life into it. If you've questioned whether you are really a writer at all, making the investment in a retreat can help you build that writer's identity.

Our lives are so precious, and so short. It's easy to fall into the thinking that we just "can't" do something out of the ordinary—especially something so "indulgent" as a writer's retreat. There are bills to pay. Family members to take care of. Jobs to tend to. Chores to be completed.

Writers tend to think about it too much. Ask the heart what it wants and it probably leaps at the idea of a writing retreat. It's the head that tries to convince us that something like that is just too selfish, difficult to afford, blah blah blah.

My writing has taken me to places I never would have gone without it—conferences, retreats, research trips, and workshops. I've never regretted a dime spent on any of them. Quite the opposite. I've grown as a writer—and a person—because of them.

So in addition to scheduling regular vacations and breaks for yourself, please add a retreat to your calendar this year. I'm positive you won't regret it. Most likely, you'll wonder why you waited so long to give yourself the gift of a few days devoted to your craft.

# PART III

# OUTWIT YOUR BRAIN'S PRODUCTIVITY SABOTEURS

BY NOW, IF you've employed even just a few of the suggestions covered in Part II, you're likely starting to see some results. You may be getting more done in less time and feeling more of a sense of accomplishment. Writing has come back into your life on a regular basis, and you're making steady progress toward your goals. You could stop here, and as long as you keep working on improving your productivity, you'd probably see some significant changes in your creative life.

But that doesn't mean the struggle is over. Maybe you did all the things we talked about, but when it was actually time to write, you didn't. Doesn't matter the reason, you just didn't. Maybe you even pulled up the file, but then couldn't get anything onto the page. You had all the best intentions, but couldn't produce anything that pleased you. Your productivity during that time was nil.

If you're still struggling with finding time to write or with actually being productive during that time, don't worry—we still have a lot of ground to cover. In this part of the book, we're going to take a look at seven things that can get in the way of your motivation to write, and that tend to reduce your writing output. These are things you might have never thought about in terms of time management and productivity, but they may be working their negative mojo on you right now without you even realizing it.

## The Unconscious Mind May be Controlling Your Behavior

The problem is that even though your conscious mind wants to produce wonderful stories during your writing time, your unconscious mind could be working against that goal. Sigmund Freud explained it like this: Think of the human mind as an iceberg. The part that sits plainly visible above water contains all the mental processes of which we are aware—our thoughts, memories, and emotions. The unconscious mind is the larger base of the iceberg that exists invisibly underwater. It is the source of dreams, intuition, impulses, instincts, thoughts, and feelings of which we're not aware.

Both the conscious and unconscious minds influence behavior, but Freud suspected the unconscious might have the upper hand because it contains hidden beliefs, fears, and attitudes. These feelings can sabotage the best intentions, leading you to do things that don't serve your highest goals.

As a creative person, you are all the more attuned to your unconscious mind and may already be aware of how it works to sabotage your writing efforts. Here's the scenario. When you dig deep into your thoughts right before you sit down with the laptop, or when you're planning out your schedule, you'll often find your mind filled with self-defeating and negative statements about your creative ability, such as:

- "I don't know why I'm doing this—I'm never going to get anywhere anyway."
- "This story is lame. I should just give up."
- "Here I am typing alone again when I should be doing something useful."
- "It's kind of stupid to spend more time on something that's just going to sit on my hard drive forever."
- "They're going to reject it anyway. Why bother?"
- "My husband/wife needed my help today. I feel guilty for writing instead."
- "This is hard…I wonder what my friends are up to on Facebook?"
- "Man, I wanted to write but I'm so tired. I think I'll take a nap."
- "I've tried and I don't know what to write next. It's like my creativity is gone."

These thoughts are often so quiet you may not even notice them, but that doesn't mean they aren't holding you back. I encourage you to really pay attention. Whenever you fail to follow through on your writing or creative time, backtrack through your thoughts to seek out the real reason why. Chances are that you're the one tripping yourself up.

## The Seven Productivity Saboteurs

It's now time to learn all the ways your mind messes with you to reduce your productivity and sabotage your creative time. They're presented here as the seven productivity saboteurs, and you must learn how to stop them in their tracks before they throw you off the trail:

1. **Writer's Guilt:** the saboteur that makes you feel guilty when you're writing, and guilty when you're not.

2. **Dis-ease:** the saboteur that when you sit down to write, makes your eyes droop, your mind go blank, and your creativity flee the premises.

3. **Self-doubt:** the saboteur that continually stops you from doing anything challenging or new.

4. **Perfectionism:** the saboteur that steals your writing time, and then when you manage to find some, paralyzes your creative mind.

5. **Workaholism:** the saboteur that keeps work at the top of your priority list, shoving writing continually to the bottom.

6. **Goal Setting:** the saboteur that ensures you'll always be perpetually discouraged.

7. **Belief:** the saboteur that fools you into thinking you must hold irrational beliefs to succeed.

Let's look at each of these individually, and see how you can outsmart its effects on your creative time, motivation, and output.

CHAPTER 12

# SABOTEUR #1—WRITER'S GUILT

MOST WRITERS EXPERIENCE writer's guilt to some extent; the real issue is how much. To find out more about the guilt you're carrying around, answer the following questions. Choose the one answer that best describes how you feel *most* of the time.

1. How do you feel when you're not finding time to write?
    a. Uneasy—like something isn't quite right in your life.
    b. Guilty—like you're leaving something important undone.
    c. Okay—you know you'll get to it eventually.
    d. Sad—like a part of you that wants to get out is being ignored.

2. How do you feel when you're actually writing?
    a. Guilty—like you should be doing something else.
    b. Selfish—like you're spending time on a selfish pursuit and should be helping others instead.
    c. Worried—like other things are being left undone.
    d. Great—you get totally lost in your work.

3. How do you feel after you've finished writing and returned to your other daily activities?
   a. Elated—like you've done what you were supposed to do.
   b. Stressed—so many things needed to be done and now you're behind.
   c. Guilty—especially when friends and loved ones express how they needed you or missed you.
   d. Concerned—like you don't know when you'll be able to fit it in again.

4. How do you feel about the overall time you've spent writing so far?
   a. Discouraged—like you don't have much to show for it.
   b. Doubtful—like you'll never make your dreams come true.
   c. Great—you've completed a number of projects and you're on your way.
   d. Guilty—like you should have been doing something else more worthwhile with your time.

5. How do you feel about the time you haven't spent writing?
   a. Sad—like you've wasted a lot of your time.
   b. Guilty—like you're not giving yourself a chance to succeed.
   c. Good—you're keeping everything balanced in your life.
   d. Discouraged—will you ever give yourself a real fighting chance to be a writer?

6. When it comes to writing (and other creative pursuits), you often feel like you:
   a. Haven't written enough.
   b. Haven't challenged yourself enough.
   c. Have let yourself down.
   d. Have done everything you could to make your dreams come true.

7. When it comes to how writing fits into the rest of your life, you feel:
   a. Like you have a good balance.
   b. Like you're always stealing time from people you care about to work on your projects.
   c. Like you're always putting yourself and your creativity last in your life.
   d. Like you just can't get everything together in a way that makes you happy.

8. What do you feel like you *should* be doing when you're writing?
   a. Cleaning house, taking care of the kids, or something more useful.
   b. Attending to all the other things in your life that need your attention.
   c. Writing! It's your writing time.
   d. Spending time with friends and family.

9. How do you feel when you don't spend time writing on any particular day?

a. Restless—like you missed an appointment.
b. Fine—you know you'll get to it the next day.
c. Guilty—like you failed to do something important.
d. Down on yourself.

10. How do you feel telling people you're a writer?
    a. Like a fraud—you don't have anything published yet.
    b. Sort of guilty—most people aren't aware of your work.
    c. Proud—it's a definite part of you.
    d. Okay, but you wish others would react more positively.

**To score:** Give yourself one point for each of these answers. Any other answer scores a "zero."

1. C
2. D
3. A
4. C
5. C
6. D
7. A
8. C
9. B
10. C

## If you scored:

**9-10 points:** Congratulations! You feel good about the time you spend writing, and you're well-balanced in how you approach it in your schedule. This likely isn't a personal saboteur for you and your writing time.

**6-8 points:** You feel torn about your writing time—good about it sometimes, guilty at others. This sneaky saboteur is weaving its way into your psyche. Keep reading to stop it from sapping your motivation to write.

**0-5 points:** You often feel guilty or selfish about taking time to write, but you may also feel guilty when you *don't* take time to write. This can have you running in circles and constantly torn about whether you should go after your dream or not. Saboteur number one is having too much fun with you.

## How Guilty Are You?

Most likely, you're carrying around some writer's guilt. If you aren't, you're in the minority. Writers and other creative artists are always seeking a happy medium. We fight the battle every day between devoting time to writing and doing regular stuff. Sometimes, we write. Sometimes, we don't. Either way, we often feel guilty, thinking that doing one thing takes time away from the other.

The emotion is so pervasive in the writing world that "writer's guilt" is a common term used to describe the feeling that you're being selfish and irresponsible spending time writing rather than doing something practical or profitable, and vice versa. This type of feeling may haunt you for two reasons:

1. You have to fit writing into your life. (Remember, there's no perfect writing life.)
2. You often have little to show in terms of income or other visible rewards for all the time spent writing.

There will always be a thousand other things you could be doing instead of writing. Writing could be viewed as the thing that takes you away from your family, children, spouse, friends, and community, and these are all important things. You may ask yourself: Why am I spending time alone making up a story when I could be doing something else important instead?

Unless you get it under control, this feeling of guilt can and will wreak havoc on your writing time. Don't let it create a vicious back-and-forth series of negative emotions that work behind the scenes to sabotage your motivation and destroy your confidence. The emotion it creates can erect an invisible force field between you and your work. That drains your creative energy. Little by little, you'll be less able to do what you feel called to do. If you don't address it, your writing will progress in fits and starts, and you'll struggle to bring your full creative self to the page.

## More Reasons for Writer's Guilt

There are many other reasons why you might feel an underlying guilt that stops you from experiencing the true joy that can come from your craft. Here are four of the most common ones.

### 1. I haven't earned much for all the time I've spent.

People tend to gauge worth in dollars. That is the way our society is. But if you're not earning money from your writing or you're earning less than a full-time wage (what most people seem to believe is the "legitimate" cut-off mark), then you risk being told that you're being self-indulgent, or you may feel that way, anyway. Since most fiction writers don't earn the equivalent of a full-time job's wages, that leaves them vulnerable to writer's guilt.

Of course, if you haven't been published yet, you face another set of issues. Maybe you've been writing for years and still haven't been able to hold your published book. Maybe you've self-published, but your books haven't sold well. Either way, you're likely to come down with a bad case of writer's guilt.

If you have no tangible rewards to show for your hard work, it can feel more like you've been wasting your time writing, particularly when you try to explain what you've been doing to friends and family—or even to yourself.

The key is to focus on the other rewards. You are a creative person. You need a creative outlet to challenge yourself and fulfill your potential. Whether or not you ever make money at writing could mean very little to your overall quality of life. You don't have to go along with society's expectations. If you agree that your life is more fulfilling when you're writing, then affirm that belief, and let go of the guilt.

**2. I don't spend enough time writing.**

You probably experience writing as a calling, which means you may also feel guilty when you're *not* writing. Even if you do get in some writing time every day, you may feel like it's not enough, or you didn't get enough words down, or you didn't focus enough during that time.

Writers are particularly hard on themselves when it comes to measuring output. If you don't produce one novel a year, or three blogs a week, or whatever your goal is, you may feel guilty about that. You may also be feeling pressured to spend any extra time you have on related tasks, like marketing. This can interfere with enjoying the time you spend with friends and family or indulging in hobbies because you're always thinking about how you should be advancing your writing career.

Don't fret. Writers have times when they're *not* writing, and those times can be difficult. If writing is your dream, don't feel that you're letting yourself down when you're not pursuing that dream. As I mentioned earlier in the book, you need downtime to restore your creative self. Enjoy it fully, and return to your work refreshed and productive.

### 3. I feel self-conscious about what I'm writing about.

It doesn't matter if you're writing a memoir or a novel, it's easy to fall into this trap. You don't want to offend anyone, but you also want your story to be as true-to-life or believable as possible.

If one of your fictional characters is based on a real person and you feel guilty about using that person in your writing, or you're writing about a topic that makes you feel uncomfortable and you can't imagine showing anyone your work, you may be filled with dread when you face that blank page. Suddenly, your project becomes the source of guilt, which makes it more difficult to focus on it completely.

Realize that you are an artist, and you are creating a work of art. Do what you need to do to avoid getting yourself into legal trouble, but then embrace your story and your subject matter. You can do your best only by giving it your all. If the work compels you, you must follow through, or you will find yourself facing writer's block caused by guilt.

## 4. I feel I'm spending too much money to become a published author.

Let's not forget feeling guilty for spending money on conferences, writer's supplies, or editing services when writing isn't covering those expenses. Even if you have a published book, you probably aren't making enough to cover all the costs for your website, professional images, blog tours, book signings, ads, and all the rest.

If this is a common source of guilt for you, take a moment to think about all the things others spend money on. Imagine your friends buying material, thread, and needles for quilting; your husband's buddies buying snowmobiles and four-wheelers for backcountry exploring; your work colleagues spending on sports equipment and remodeling projects. Certainly you can qualify your creative work as something worthwhile investing in. After all, even if you never make a dime, you're learning a skill and bettering yourself. Can all your friends and acquaintances say that?

### Decide to Make Peace with Your Choices

One other type of general writer's guilt that you may be battling with is the kind that hides out in your subconscious, nagging you on a regular basis for no particular reason. It can drag you down and make it harder for you to reach your writing goals. It's that unseen part of the iceberg sending cold thoughts up into your conscious mind: "This is going to make you feel guilty, so best not do it," or "You shouldn't be wasting your time on this," or "Why haven't you spent more time on this?" If you feel guilty about the whole endeavor, your brain may decide that it's better to avoid it entirely.

In the regular world, guilt can be a constructive emotion if it compels you to take action. Feeling guilty about hurting someone's feelings can motivate you to make amends, which in turn, can improve your relationship. What writers usually feel guilty about, though, has nothing to do with doing anything "wrong." Instead, it's all about the choices we make, and making peace with those choices.

Decide today to allow yourself to gain joy from your writing. Realize that you are not superhuman. Your choices will not be infallible. Do the best you can, and let it be. Fully accept writing as a part of your life—not something you can decide is important one day and not the next. Commit to your creative self and accept the consequences. Chances are, this creative part of your being is not going away any time soon, so it's best to make peace with the reality that you must make room for it and not feel guilty.

---

### Time Treasure

## Ten Ways to Ease Writer's Guilt

As you work to make more room for writing in your schedule, commit yourself to easing your writer's guilt. Be on notice that this type of guilt may never go away completely, but you can lessen its impact on your thoughts and emotions and loosen its hold on your creativity with these suggestions:

1. **Compare writing to the other things you do.** Cleaning

the bathroom, watching an hour of TV, going out with friends, getting a haircut, or playing a game of baseball—chances are, you do these things and many more. They could all be considered a lot less "productive" than writing, yet you probably don't have any guilt about doing them. So when you feel guilty about writing, compare it to other activities and reassure yourself how worthwhile your writing time is.

2. **Realize how easy it is to "waste time."** When sitting at your writing desk—especially if you haven't been published yet—it's easy to worry that you're "wasting your time." Consider for a moment what wasting time really is. According to a survey by Salary.com, the average company employee spends 1.7 hours a day on non-productive activities, including socializing, surfing the net, and taking long breaks. If you're writing, you're being productive. Instead of worrying about wasting time, congratulate yourself for spending that time working toward your dream.

3. **Imagine what else you would do with your time.** If you didn't write, what else would you do? Honestly, would you be happier with the results next week, or even ten, twenty, or thirty years from now if you did something else instead? Writing yields long-term rewards, but you need to stick with it.

4. **Money isn't everything.** Instead of focusing strictly on

activities that provide external rewards (such as money and position), focus on the fact that a balanced life involves activities like writing that provide intrinsic rewards—that give you pleasure, and help you find meaning.

5. **Look inside yourself for answers.** If you resent agreeing to spend less time writing, you need to rethink that decision. On the other hand, if you think you're a better person when you sacrifice what you'd rather do to please someone else, then do that. The point is that you must do what feels best for you, not what you think you "should" do.

6. **Realize that writing is good for you.** You know that eating right, exercising, and getting a good night's sleep are all good for your body (and mind!), but what you may not realize is that spending time on creative work is good for you emotionally. As a creative being, committing to writing on a regular basis is just as important to your health as eating a balanced diet. Make sure to include writing in the same category as other good-for-you activities.

7. **Keep a daily journal.** Give yourself some real data to work with by keeping a journal of your writing time (or lack of it) and how you feel about it for at least a week. This is really useful if you're worried about spending too much or too little time on writing. It will help you examine exactly how you're spending your time so you can take

appropriate action. If you're truly neglecting your family, for example, the proof will be in your journal.

8. **Remember you're not perfect.** You may try to be a perfect parent, spouse, caretaker, employee, business owner, and writer all at the same time. But trying to be perfect is not only a losing battle, it will perpetuate your cycle of guilt. Break the cycle by learning to forgive yourself, and use every day as an excuse to start fresh.

9. **Realize when others are manipulating you.** Writing is important to you, so don't be manipulated with statements like, "You're just being selfish writing all the time." Check in with your guilt and take action if needed, but otherwise hold to your writing commitments and don't allow others to make you feel badly. You don't have to ignore friends and family. Simply say, "I'll call you back at 3:00, when my writing time is over." Better yet, let them leave a message.

10. **Make peace with your choices.** This one is worth repeating. Pursuing your writing dream is a choice. How you go about fulfilling that dream is also a choice. Trust yourself to make the right decisions. You are obviously compelled to write, so it's best not to ignore this calling. Make the choices you need to make, and be brave enough to commit to them wholeheartedly—without guilt.

CHAPTER 13

# SABOTEUR #2—DIS-EASE

When I was in my mid-thirties, I experienced a high volume of work in my freelance business. Freelancers understand the natural ebb and flow that goes with the job. When we're fortunate enough to get an influx of clients and/or projects, we usually tend to make hay while the sun shines, so to speak, because we know that things can slow down just as quickly.

So I was working, and working hard. I sat at my computer day and night pounding out articles, brochures, booklets, website copy, and reports, and ghostwrote a book on the side. When I wasn't working I was either teaching music lessons or playing horn in some group or other, which translated to a lot of sitting.

I usually spent about thirty minutes a night doing yoga—something I'd committed to in my twenties to offset running injuries—but didn't have time for a lot of other daily exercise. I did jog at least a couple times a week, though, and considered myself to be in "good" shape because I wasn't overweight and was quite flexible.

Over time, however, my back started to get sore. I didn't think much about it, figuring it would go away when the work let up. Well the work didn't let up and I continued for months at a pretty crazy pace. Then, one weekend, it all came back to bite me.

I was cleaning house on a Saturday, and I distinctly remember bending down by one of the easy chairs in the living room to pick something up off the floor. Suddenly I was seized by what I can only describe as "lightning-bolt" pain across my entire lower back. It felt like what I imagine it might feel like to be tased by a police officer. I fell onto the floor, in pain and confused. It's not like I'd just tried to lift 200 pounds or something. After I got over the initial shock I tried to move, but any movement at all brought the pain back, sharp and powerful. I waited, sure it would pass, but after about twenty minutes I started to get concerned.

What had I done?

It was another couple hours before I was able to get myself to my hands and knees. I spent the rest of the weekend either on the floor or crawling around. It soon became clear that I had suffered a back injury, somehow, though just *how* totally escaped me.

A week passed before I was mobile enough to go to the doctor, who gave me a prescription for pain and referred me to a spine specialist. Meanwhile, I relied on my yoga and a series of very slow and easy stretches to gradually increase my mobility.

Despite my progress, there was one thing I found near impossible to do—work. Sitting at the computer was out of the question, and it was very difficult to try to think through an article while in pain. I finally transferred everything to a portable hard drive and worked lying on the floor with the laptop perched on my stomach.

I continued this way for a couple months until I was able to recover enough to get back into my office chair. The saddest part was that my own creative writing had to be put aside. Talk about heartbreaking.

The spine specialist diagnosed me as having suffered a herniated disc, but assured me my yoga and other exercises were working, and surgery was unnecessary (thank heavens).

What did I learn from all this?

> *If I wanted to spend time writing, I had to take care of myself.*

## The Importance of Feeling Good

Your world turns because you make it turn. If you're pulled out of commission because of an injury or an illness—or just because you aren't operating at optimal levels—your ability to get things done is severely compromised. Sometimes, things even come to a complete halt. So much for finding time to write.

Productivity saboteur #2—dis-ease—can rob you of your writing time in a snap. Dis-ease of any kind, from a mild headache to a full-blown illness or injury, saps your resources. Think of how much you normally accomplish in a day, from getting up and showering to getting dressed and eating breakfast, running daily errands and taking care of those around you, managing the stress and surprises in your life, and doing it all over again day after day.

Accomplishing even the minimum takes loads of energy. To keep up, you have to be operating at normal speed at the very least. Adding an intense activity like writing to your daily routine means you're looking to do more than that. You don't want to just keep up, you need to clear the way to do more. That means you need to become more productive, and trust me—*how productive you are depends entirely on how good you feel*.

To maintain the machine that is your body and mind, you need to focus on three main areas of self-care:

1. safeguard your energy,
2. keep your brain sharp, and
3. relieve stress.

## A. SAFEGUARD YOUR ENERGY

Even if you're just a little tired, you're going to find it harder to stick with your writing commitment. Fatigue makes it more likely you'll succumb to distractions, or stare at the blank page and then pick up your smartphone "just to check." Weariness also makes it harder to focus. The weary mind wanders and spaces out. Sleep deprivation impairs attention, working memory, and decision-making, and also reduces creativity. In 2010, researchers reported that "more creative, divergent and innovative aspects of cognition do appear to be degraded by lack of sleep."

If you do actually manage to write when you're tired, you probably won't be happy with the result. Tired writing is often uninspired writing. When I'm tired and force myself to write anyway, I tend to fall back on standard descriptions and simplistic scene directions that later read as boring and amateurish—definitely not my best work. You're likely to do the same thing when your brain is sluggish and weary.

If you're not convinced that fatigue negatively affects your writing, keep a sleep log for a week or two. Record how many hours of sleep you get per night, the quality of sleep (restless or sound), and how much energy you have (or don't have) during the day. Then take a look at the writing you completed during that time—the proof will be there.

If you're not the type to keep a journal, get an activity tracker.

Not only will it help you to be more active during the day by tracking your steps, but if you get the more advanced model, it will also keep an accurate record of your sleep patterns.

> **Time Treasure**
>
> ## Get More Sleep
>
> Lack of sleep is a common complaint these days, but it's easily remedied if you follow these tips to reach the recommended seven to eight hours a night:
>
> - **Ban electronics from the bedroom:** This means smartphones, tablets, computers, handheld game consoles, and televisions. They emit blue light, which messes with your sleep hormones and destroys your circadian rhythms. (The exception is an e-reader that doesn't have a backlight.) In addition, stop using them all at least an hour before bed.
>
> - **Keep the bedroom cool and dark:** We sleep better in cooler environments. Light of any kind signals the brain it's time to wake up, so limit night lights, draw the shades, and wear an eye mask if needed.
>
> - **Invest in a good mattress:** Don't skimp on the mattresses. This, like your writing chair, is where you need to splurge. Get a good quality mattress that supports you and you'll wake up rested and refreshed.

- **Keep regular hours:** Try to go to bed and wake up at about the same time every day, even on weekends. A regular routine will set your inner clock and improve your quality of sleep.

- **Avoid caffeine and alcohol before bed:** Caffeine can keep you awake. Alcohol may make you sleepy initially, but will disrupt your "deep" sleep later on, which is what you really need to feel refreshed the next morning.

## B. KEEP YOUR BRAIN SHARP

You've probably heard of "brain fog." It's that dull kind of feeling that makes it difficult to remember things and leaves you generally a little slow on the uptake. It can also render your writing time useless.

You may already know this from experience. You sit down to write after work, but your brain is just "fuzzy." You can't think straight, you can't remember what your characters were doing in an earlier scene, and you can't come up with a new scene to save your life. It's very frustrating.

The main cures for brain fog are:

- Eat a better diet.
- Get more exercise.

I can hear you groaning already, and I'm not here to make you feel guilty. My goal is to help you get at least thirty minutes of exercise a day and eat more whole foods (and less fast food and processed food) to improve your physical health, boost your creativity, clear your brain fog, and give you more energy to write.

You have to see yourself as the creative machine you are. You wouldn't attempt to run your car without a good, quality fuel and expect to get very far. Yet you may grab fast food or salty snacks on the run, sit at the desk all day without exercise, and expect to function at top form. You're not that different from your car. You need the right fuel and the right care to perform optimally.

## Choose Healthier Foods

Let's start with your diet. We all know that foods high in fat, salt, and sugar (like fast foods, fried foods, and processed foods) are bad for our health, but recent studies show they also affect the brain. In 2015, researchers reported that diets high in sugar or fat impaired memory and cognitive flexibility. (Sugar created worse results than fat, by the way.)

Diets high in saturated fat (such as that found in fried foods and processed foods) also slowed brain functioning, and compelled participants to want to eat *more* fatty foods, which only made the problem worse. (Healthy fats, such as olive oil and avocados, don't cause the same problems as unhealthy fats, and are actually beneficial for you in small amounts.) Inhaling a fast-food lunch, for example, will have you dragging through your afternoon, your productivity plummeting as you try to complete your projects for the day.

To avoid the fast-food rush, try to plan your meals ahead of time. Stack your house, office, and car with healthy snack options. Pack your lunch or order healthy items. The more focused attention you can bring to your diet, the more successful you'll be. In general, think more fruits, veggies, whole grains, low-fat dairy, and lean (not processed) meats.

Sugar, perhaps even more than fat, can kill your creative mojo. Scientists have found that participants eating a diet high in high fructose corn syrup (which is in so many common foods these days) showed actual damage in their brains. A high-sugar diet can also increase risk of mood disorders, anxiety, and depression—something we creative types definitely don't need help with!

**If sugar is a strong issue for you, be aware that it can be addictive.** Recent studies have shown that it's just as addictive as cocaine and other drugs. That means the more you eat it, the more you want it. Be aware of your own feelings. If you find that your cravings are getting out of hand, cut back. A trick: when a craving comes on, drink a nice tall glass of water. It helps.

Snacking is an area where writers need to be particularly careful. We tend to mindlessly eat while writing, which can sabotage the brain, particularly if we're gnawing on chips, cookies, and candy. Go for nuts, yogurt, whole-grain crackers, a green smoothie, cut-up fruits or veggies, a small piece of 70% cocoa dark chocolate, or a cup of tea.

The bottom line is if you want to maintain optimal productivity and bring all of your creative powers to the page, you need to watch what you eat.

### Move More!

We are all capable of coming up with the best excuses for why we can't exercise more than we do. I may be a health writer, but I'm no big fan of running the treadmill myself. Exercise for exercise's sake is tough for most of us, as it seems like we could be doing something more *useful* with our time…like writing.

How's this for motivation: Exercise keeps the brain alert, creativity sharp, and energy high, which means you'll be much more able to stick with your writing routine.

People tell me they're "too tired" to exercise. I chuckle to myself because the truth of it is, if you're tired, you need to exercise more. Exercise creates energy. In fact, in 2006, researchers found that regular exercise was *more effective* against chronic fatigue than medications, such as the narcolepsy drug modafinil:

"We live in a society where people are always looking for the next sports drink, energy bar or cup of coffee that will give them the extra edge to get through the day," said lead study author Tim Puetz. "But it may be that lacing up your tennis shoes and getting out and doing some physical activity every morning can provide that spark of energy that people are looking for."

A later 2008 study found that regular, low-intensity exercise helped reduce fatigue by 65 percent. That's a lot!

I've found this to be true in my own life. When I start dragging through my days, nine times out of ten it's because I've been neglecting my exercise. Usually just getting in a thirty-minute walk is enough to help me bounce back.

Getting your heartbeat going can also boost creativity. Take, for example, a group of college students who took a creativity test either after aerobic exercise or after being sedentary—exercise significantly increased creative potential, even after a two-hour lag time.

In addition to recommitting to your daily exercise routine, it's also important to move more throughout the day. It will help you keep your energy up and your brain firing on all cylinders. Get up every half hour from the desk. Stand up to take phone calls. Print out your materials so you can walk when editing a story. Use a small water glass and get up to refill it more often. Find excuses to move, move, move.

Time Treasure

## Use Exercise to Supercharge your Writing Time

Instead of thinking of exercise as something you have to add to your "to-do" list, make it a companion to your writing time. While jogging, let your mind wander through your next scene, or listen to an audio book about writing. Take your cell phone with you on your walk and use a voice-recording app to get your ideas down as you go.

Walking is one of the best exercises you can do as a writer, by the way, and has been popular among many of the greats. In *How to Write Science Fiction and Fantasy* (1990), novelist Orson Scott Card suggested that it's "worth the time to take an hour's walk before writing. You may write a bit less for the time spent, but you may find that you write better."

Studies have found that brainpower is actually increased *while walking*, suggesting that the activity itself is a way to boost your ability to think through a plot problem or unearth a character's deeply held secrets.

Hemingway was fond of walking as a way of working out issues in his writing. "I would walk along the quais when I had finished work or when I was trying to think something out," he wrote in *A Moveable Feast*. "It was easier to think if I was walking and doing something or seeing people doing something that they understood."

> Whatever exercise works best for you, see if you can use it to let your mind wander creatively to inspire your writing. If you can see exercise as an important partner in reaching your writing goals, you'll notice big boosts in your productivity.

## C. RELIEVE STRESS

Stress leads to a number of physical problems like headaches, chronic inflammation, depression, digestive disorders, and more. Unfortunately, it also messes with your ability to be creative.

The higher the stress level, the lower the creativity, scientists say. After reviewing 9,000 daily diary entries from people who were working on projects that required high levels of creativity, they found that stress, in the form of time pressure, resulted in less creative results.

"When creativity is under the gun," the authors wrote, "it usually ends up getting killed."

Stress also blocks the ability to come up with new ideas. As a creative person, you know that your work depends on your ability to think up new scenarios. Rats need to be able to do that too, when figuring out when to press a lever for food, but in a 2009 study, those who were chronically stressed could no longer think in their usual cunning way. Instead, they fell back on familiar routines and rote responses—the exact opposite of being creative. They kept doing the same things and getting the same results, rather than figuring out what they needed to do instead to get the reward. (Sound familiar?) It was so bad that there were actual detectable changes in the brain. Areas associated with goal-directed behaviors shriveled, while those associated with habit formation flourished.

When stress hijacks our higher brain functions, we revert to habitual responses. Learning, memory, attention span, and our ability to focus are all affected.

Think about when you do your best writing. Most likely, it's when you're able to sink into that creative zone, relax, and let your brain waves slow down enough to allow you to enter that other world where your characters live. This doesn't happen when you're stressed.

Even viewing a stressful video clip—such as a scene from *Saving Private Ryan* vs. a scene from *Shrek*—was found to affect creative thinking. Those who viewed the less stressful *Shrek* scene answered correctly on a word-association task thirty-nine percent more often than those who watched the more stressful *Saving Private Ryan* scene.

As you can see, stress is very damaging to creative ability, so you need to find a way to relieve it to make your writing time more productive.

---

### Time Treasure

## Practice a Daily Stress-Relieving Activity

There's no way to completely eliminate stress from your life, but you can learn to manage it more effectively and to keep it from interfering with your writing time. Here are some tips to help you do that:

1. **Get creative.** Of course, if you're stressed to begin with, you're likely to have trouble writing, so turn to another less challenging creative pursuit instead. Knitting and

crocheting, doing crafts, painting, drawing, playing a musical instrument, scrapbooking, woodworking, and even gardening can all do the trick.

2. **Do something that makes you happy.** A positive brain is a creative brain. That means you need to do something to get happy again. Get away for the weekend, go out for a nice dinner, listen to your favorite music, spend time with a pet, or talk with a close friend. Allow yourself the so-called "luxury." It's important for your own self-care.

3. **Find a daily stress-relieving activity.** If you don't have a stress-relieving activity that you do *every day*, it's time to get one. It's critical to your health, creativity, and well-being. Yoga, tai chi, meditation, art therapy, counseling, sports, dancing, journaling, coloring (a popular trend!), and deep breathing all work. Any relaxing activity you enjoy will do, just commit to doing it regularly.

4. **Eat healthy.** A diet rich in fruits, vegetables, beans, nuts, and olive oil (the "Mediterranean diet") helps boost feel-good brain neurotransmitters and reduces the risk of depression. Foods with the calming amino-acid tryptophan—like turkey, nuts, eggs, oats, fish, and beans—increase happiness and well-being while reducing feelings of irritability. Yogurt is another good choice as the probiotics help balance the brain-gut connection. One study even found that women who ate

yogurt handled stress better than those who didn't. Or you can sit down with a nice cup of tea. It typically has less caffeine than coffee, and contains healthy antioxidants that can reduce anxiety and promote calm.

5. **Move.** In addition to all the benefits we talked about above, exercise helps relieve stress. In fact, it may be the best option available. It naturally produces feel-good endorphins in the brain and helps you sleep, which is often difficult when you're stressed. Exercise also elevates mood—that positive feeling you need to create. It even helps "train the brain" to better manage stress. A study out of Princeton University found that regular exercise changed the brain so it reacted less negatively to stress.

## Healthy Writers Are Productive Writers

If you can manage the three main obstacles to your creative work—fatigue, brain fog, and stress—you'll have more energy, be more productive, and sustain your motivation to write and get more done. If your goal is to be a successful writer, you must take care of yourself. That means listening to your body. If something hurts, stop what you're doing and try to fix it. If you're tired, find a way to get more rest and exercise. When you're hungry, make the choice to eat good, wholesome, and nutritious foods.

We all have unique physiologies and react differently to our environments. You have to find what works for you. The hard part is giving yourself permission to take the time you need to take care of yourself.

If your creative work is important to you, you can't do it well if your body and mind are malfunctioning. You are the machine that produces the materials. You are the energy behind the projects. You are the magic wand that creates the story.

You must operate at optimal levels for your work to shine.

Don't let the saboteur dis-ease mess with your writing progress. Put self-care first on your list. When you feel well, see if you don't magically start fitting more productive writing time into your life.

---

Time Treasure

## Commit to One New Self-Care Activity

Commit to one new self-care activity this week. Examples may include:

- signing up for a new yoga class,

- making a regular appointment with a friend to go for a walk,

- changing your daily lunch to something more healthy,

- going shopping for more nutritious snacks,

- trying a new stress-relieving craft,

- making an appointment for a weekly massage,

- or finding a new, more comfortable mattress.

Write down your new self-care activity below. What will you do this week to take care of yourself?

_____

_____

## CHAPTER 14

# SABOTEUR #3—SELF-DOUBT

I'D LIKE YOU to take another short quiz. Answer the questions as honestly as you can, based on how you *really feel* down deep inside, not on how you think you "should" feel. It's important that you're truthful, because this simple quiz will give you key insights into the way you're feeling about yourself and your creative work.

1. When I receive a rejection or when someone doesn't like my work, I feel like a failure and I'm very hard on myself.
   a. Never
   b. Hardly ever
   c. Sometimes
   d. Quite often
   e. Always

2. I worry that people will think negatively of my writing and creative projects.
   a. Never
   b. Hardly ever
   c. Sometimes
   d. Quite often

e. Always

3. If I'm not progressing on my project, I get easily frustrated.

   a. Never

   b. Hardly ever

   c. Sometimes

   d. Quite often

   e. Always

4. I often sacrifice my creative time for others who ask me to do things for them.

   a. Never

   b. Hardly ever

   c. Sometimes

   d. Quite often

   e. Always

5. I secretly believe I'm not as "good" or as "talented" as others think I am.

   a. Never

   b. Hardly ever

   c. Sometimes

   d. Quite often

   e. Always

6. In the middle of a writing project, I often feel like it's not very good, and doubt my ability to make it live up to what I hoped it could be.

   a. Never

b. Hardly ever

c. Sometimes

d. Quite often

e. Always

7. Despite my accomplishments as a creative person, I still worry that soon, people will discover the (unflattering) truth about my talent (or lack thereof).

a. Never

b. Hardly ever

c. Sometimes

d. Quite often

e. Always

8. I know I have an amazing book (or painting or sculpture or other creative project) in me, but I'm afraid to tell anyone that.

a. Never

b. Hardly ever

c. Sometimes

d. Quite often

e. Always

9. When facing a critique or review, I brace for the worst.

a. Never

b. Hardly ever

c. Sometimes

d. Quite often

e. Always

10. I have a gut feeling about my work and what direction it should take, but it's difficult to trust my instincts, especially when they go against what I've been taught or what others (like mentors, teachers, readers, or editors) tell me.

    a. Never
    b. Hardly ever
    c. Sometimes
    d. Quite often
    e. Always

To score your quiz, assign each answer the following points:

A = 5
B = 4
C = 3
D = 2
E = 1

Your total: _____

**What Your Score Means**

**40-50:** Lucky you! You feel confident and sure of your creative instincts.
**30-40:** Like most creative people, you experience self-doubt. This is normal and you're not alone.
**20-30:** Your self-doubt is seriously hampering your creative activities. You need to take action soon so it doesn't become a self-fulfilling prophecy.
**0–20:** If you don't take action now, your self-doubt will stop you in your creative tracks. You need to develop faith in your creative instincts.

## Challenge Those Feelings of Self-Doubt

There are few other things in life that can sabotage your creative efforts quite like self-doubt can. It's devious, destructive, and extremely detrimental to your writing dreams (or to any dreams, for that matter). It will make you second-guess yourself, slow your progress, and may even stop you completely if you let it.

You can go for years *intending* to write but never get anything done because self-doubt is silently sabotaging you at every turn. You can also succeed at publishing a number of successful books, but still secretly worry that you're not *really* a good writer because self-doubt cancels all the evidence to the contrary.

It's that bad.

When I look back on over twenty-five years of writing, I see long periods of little progress interspersed with big spikes in creative achievement. Those spikes happened when I managed to overcome self-doubt and approach my work with confidence. I know now that if I had tackled this emotion earlier, I would have progressed more quickly.

Starting today, you need to see self-doubt as the enemy it is. I suggest picturing it as a snake, since most people have a negative view of snakes. Besides, it starts with an "s," so it makes it easy to remember. From here on out, we're dealing with:

The Self-Doubt Snake (or SDS as it's known in more familiar circles).

I picture the SDS curling itself around my writing dreams and choking the life out of them. Mine is a boa-style snake, and trust me, it's just as dangerous. Hold onto that image for a few minutes and see if it resonates with you. If it does, the next time you feel a wave of self-doubt coming on, you can identify it as the SDS, and act swiftly to challenge its presence in your creative world.

## Ten Ways the SDS Sabotages Writing Dreams

This slithering saboteur affects your life in more ways than you probably imagined, and wreaks havoc at every stage of the creative process. Here are just a few examples of how it works:

1. **Instills doubt.** When you sit down to write, the SDS is often there by your side. Any time you doubt whether you can fill the blank page, complete the project, or write at all, that's the SDS hissing in your ear. When you experience the feeling of "I can't" because of reason x, y, or z, that's self-doubt putting the death squeeze on your writing goals.

2. **Makes you feel "less than."** If you've been in a writer's group and felt like you had to duck your head because you weren't as good or as smart or as talented, that was the SDS inhibiting your self-confidence and causing you to miss out on participating as an equal.

3. **Makes it easy for others to use you.** Self-doubt stops you from standing up for yourself. It makes you avoid explaining to your family that you need time to write, or asking your employer for the weekend off, or saying "no" to friends when their requests interfere with your writing schedule.

4. **Makes you put others' goals before your own.** Self-doubt makes you believe your goals and dreams come last, after you've attended to everyone else's. The result is that you have less time to devote to your creative work, and you progress more slowly, if at all.

5. **Stops you from taking action.** When you doubt yourself, you wait. Say your intuition whispers that it's time to cut back

on your work hours so you can take your writing career to the next level. The SDS will bring up all your fears about that idea. It will cause you to imagine the worst possible outcome (rather than the best) and convince you that you won't be able to handle the consequences if the boss balks. This paralyzes you with fear, so you won't take that step forward, and everything will stay just as it is in your life—your dreams will go nowhere.

6. **Keeps you in your "place."** The SDS is really good at this. It likes to keep you right where you are. No thinking big, dreaming big, or being more than you are now is allowed. Every time you want to improve your life, rearrange your schedule to give yourself more creative time, delegate some of your tasks, or make any other productive improvements, the SDS will raise its ugly head and say, "Who do you think you are? That will never work. Be grateful for what you have and quit being so selfish."

7. **Stops others from taking you seriously.** When you doubt yourself, you'll find that others will doubt you, too. A lack of confidence is something you can't hide. It shows up in your sloppy posture, low energy, lack of eye contact, and even in your tone of voice. So if you go to that writer's conference with the SDS firmly wrapped around you, you'll unconsciously bow your head, cave your shoulders in, and speak mutedly, transmitting a clear message that tells others not to take you seriously.

8. **Makes you doubt your instincts.** As a creative person, you need your instincts. They save you. They guide each project

you do, helping you to choose one scene over the other or to switch to a different setting. They also help you to decide when to take the next career leap, or when it's best to step out of your comfort zone. The SDS makes you question your instincts, and over time, will cause you to stop trusting them altogether. Say a new thought pops into your head that you should try writing in another genre. The SDS will shut it down. It will bring up all the reasons why you aren't "ready" for such a step, and why the market will ignore you. It will encourage you to ask someone else about it, because surely you aren't smart enough or experienced enough to make the right decision. When you do, the SDS will make you appear doubtful and unsure. The other person will sense that doubt, and likely agree with your SDS—that maybe this isn't a good idea right now. Even if the other person encourages you, your SDS will slant the advice so it dovetails with what the SDS is telling you. As a result, you'll put aside what may have been a great idea. Score another one for the SDS. This scenario is especially true when receiving critiques of your work. You will have instincts about which comments apply and which don't. You should listen to them, but the SDS will encourage you to give equal weight to them all, and to listen to everyone else's opinion first, until you become completely confused about what to do with your work, sometimes to the point of abandoning it.

9. **Discourages you from trying new things.** Every time you try something new, you have to learn something new. Obviously you aren't going to know everything you need to know

when embarking on a new project. Yet the SDS will convince you that this is unacceptable. "You want to write in a new genre? You've never written in that genre before. It won't work. You don't know what you're doing." This same thought process will haunt any attempt to branch out and expand your abilities and skills.

10. **Distorts how you see yourself.** You could be an amazing writer, artist, speaker, marketer, entrepreneur, and overall creative master, but the SDS will never allow you to believe that. It will keep you constantly questioning your instincts, your abilities, and your creative desires so that your progress is sporadic, at best.

## Self-Doubt Is Extremely Common

After being around creative people (writers, musicians, artists) for most of my life, I've learned that we all feel self-doubt at one time or another, usually more often than we'd like. The good news is that if you're feeling self-doubt, you're in good company, because most people who do have a deep understanding of quality art.

I once met an older gentleman at a writer's conference who was a very accomplished painter. This guy had traveled the world, been featured in galleries everywhere, and won numerous awards. Yet when I handed him my business card, the first thing he noticed was the "self-doubt" icon I had printed on the back.

"I could use your help with this one," he said, pointing to the icon. "I've struggled with that all my life."

I was shocked. This man appeared confident and self-assured. Well dressed, funny, and personable, in the eyes of his colleagues, he had arrived. I had assumed that surely someone of his caliber would have put self-doubt behind him, but I was wrong.

I now know that this isn't uncommon. Even successful Hollywood actress Cameron Diaz said that self-doubt nearly paralyzed her before the publication of her book, *The Body Book: Feed, Move, Understand and Love Your Amazing Body.* "People" magazine reported that Diaz shared her feelings at an event in West Hollywood:

"I realized I was just so scared that I was going to put this thing into the world and everybody's going to see me, and what if they don't like me? What if they think I'm crazy or I'm stupid?"

We writers know how frightening it is to publish a book and wonder what people will think of it. Most of us wouldn't expect that a famous actress like Cameron Diaz would experience self-doubt, but her comments make it plain that the SDS doesn't discriminate.

Meryl Streep, too, one of the most lauded actresses of our time, is quoted as saying, "You think, 'Why would anyone want to see me again in a movie? And I don't know how to act anyway, so why am I doing this?'"

Bestselling author and creativity guru Steven Pressfield (*War of Art*) went through what he calls "panic attacks" when working on his novel, *The Lion's Gate:* "I'm consumed with dread and feelings of inadequacy. What if I can't make this project work? What if I fail? What if I get into these interviews and my mind goes blank?"

Nobel Laureate Maya Angelou said, "I have written eleven books, but each time I think, 'uh oh, they're going to find out now. I've run a game on everybody, and they're going to find me out.'"

So you see, you're in good company. Countless numbers of famous, accomplished people also had to deal with self-doubt over the course of their careers, yet they didn't let it stop them.

## Notice the SDS's Predictable Pattern, Call it Out, and Take Action

To rob the SDS of its stifling power, all you have to do is take notice of its predictable pattern. It operates the same way every time. You may not be aware of that yet, but if you start paying attention, you'll notice it. In general, it does its work in three stages:

1. **Trigger:** Something triggers the SDS to appear.
2. **Habitual response:** You respond by habit, experiencing negative emotions because of what the SDS says.
3. **Give up:** You give up on your idea or on yourself.

First, something causes the SDS to slither out of its hole in the ground. Common triggers include trying something new, stretching yourself, facing a challenging creative project, or getting out of your comfort zone. Other triggers include comparing yourself to other artists, receiving a critique, or failing to get something you wanted, like a publishing contract or recognition in a contest.

These and other similar activities will trigger the SDS to appear and start squeezing the air out of your lungs. It will rise up and hiss in your ear: "You can't do this! I told you this was a dumb idea. You need to stop now before you embarrass yourself."

Next time you have that feeling of self-doubt, stop and figure out what you've done to trigger the SDS. Determine what you were thinking, doing, or imagining that could have sparked those thoughts. If you take note every time it happens, you'll start to see a pattern.

*Try something new. Feel challenged. Think doubting thoughts.*

Or…

*Get a writing critique. Feel confused. Think doubting thoughts.*

The problem is you usually just accept your doubting thoughts as truths. They appear to be logical, after all. You submitted to that contest and failed to place, so you must not be a very good writer. You tried writing in a new genre and struggled with it, so obviously it was a dumb decision. You fall hook, line, and sinker for all those icky emotions, believing you have no talent, you'll never achieve your goals, and you were stupid and selfish to try anything new in the first place.

Spotting the pattern will help rob the SDS of some of its power. You'll notice these thoughts aren't necessarily true, they're just habitual. They show up in response to certain triggers. Once you realize this, your next step is to call out the SDS: "I see you. I know what you're trying to do, and I'm not going to let you succeed." Just bringing it into the light will make it appear a lot less menacing.

Finally, you have only to take action. Vincent Van Gogh is quoted as saying, "If you hear a voice within you say 'you cannot paint,' then by all means paint, and that voice will be silenced."

If you *do* exactly what the SDS says you can't do, you'll shut it up in a hurry. When you take action—any action, even a small one—you'll move forward, and you'll leave the SDS behind. Small actions involve little risk, and are therefore easier to manage.

So in summary, to rob the SDS of its power, you have only to:

1. **Recognize the trigger:** Go back and figure out what triggered the SDS to emerge in the first place.

2. **Realize you responded out of habit:** Become aware that

your negative emotions are there only because you have a habit of listening to the SDS.

3. **Take action:** Take some positive action toward your goal, and rob the SDS of its power.

Let's say your inner voice is telling you to cut back on your work hours so you have more time to write, but the SDS has convinced you that your boss will think less of you and eventually fire you if you follow through on this idea.

Instead of holding back, take a small step in the direction your intuition wants to go. Maybe you can start by leaving fifteen minutes earlier, then use that time to write in your car before you actually drive away. When you see that you haven't been axed after the first week, increase the time to twenty minutes. Drive somewhere nearby, park, and write.

Each time you take a small step toward your goal and discover the SDS only spouted lies, you gain power. It's like winning gold coins in a video game. Ka-ching! Suddenly you have more confidence with which to take your next step—maybe adding fifteen minutes to your lunch break to write, or refusing to be available to your job by cell phone on a Sunday.

## Time Treasure

## **Subdue Your Self-Doubt**

In addition to implementing the three-step process described above, you can use other methods to subdue your self-doubt.

- **Get into the habit of writing regularly.** If you commit to writing for thirty minutes every morning before work, and the SDS starts telling you you're not getting anywhere, you can easily ignore it because frankly, it doesn't matter. You have created a habit, which makes it much easier to stick with it regardless of what the SDS says. Habit goes a long way toward defeating this snake.

- **Give yourself a pep talk.** If you're going to a writer's conference but feel insecure about your identity as a writer because you haven't published anything or because you'll be around writers who have accomplished more than you, give yourself a pep talk before the event. Remember that your intent is not to impress everyone else, but to learn, network, or get an agent. Focus on what you need to do to accomplish your goals, and tell yourself you are just as valued a member of that conference as all the other attendees.

- **Ignore the SDS.** Self-doubt has a habit of going away if you ignore it. "Yeah, yeah, here it comes again." This sort of attitude helps you deflate the emotion, particularly if you remind yourself that it's showing up because of its predictable pattern. *I'm going to a conference where I'm going to be around other experienced writers, so of course, here comes the SDS to make me feel insecure. I'm just going to ignore it and focus on learning everything I can.*

- **Act "as if."** This is one of the most effective ways of dealing with the SDS at any time, for any occasion. Pick someone you admire—a writer, painter, musician, or even a fictional character. Ask yourself how she would act in this situation, how she would approach other writers and conduct herself overall. Pull up YouTube videos of your heroes. Watch and copy their movements, so that when you find yourself in a similar situation, you have something to model yourself on. Act confident and self-assured, even if you aren't. People can only judge you by the persona you project. Try it! The result will be nothing less than magical.

## Make Peace with the SDS

On a final note, if you think that one day you'll be good enough, skilled enough, creative enough, accomplished enough, or whatever to ditch self-doubt, think again. You care about your art and about being the best you can be, so you will have to make peace with the fact that the SDS is likely to stick around.

The trick is to make peace with that, and to use the coping mechanisms you've learned here to be less vulnerable to the SDS's "charms." Notice the trigger, call the beast out, and take action. The more you do this, the less self-doubt will paralyze you. Even if it still does show up on occasion, you'll be able to move forward in spite of it.

The important thing is not to let self-doubt slow you down. When it hisses in your ear, turn on some music and keep writing.

CHAPTER 15

# SABOTEUR #4— PERFECTIONISM

A FRIEND OF MINE has written a novel. I have a feeling it's a good novel. I've read part of it, though he won't allow me to read it all. He's still fixing some things, he says. The problem is, he's been saying that for ten years.

I didn't see anything that needed to be fixed in the part I read. In fact, I encouraged him to submit it to editors or agents. But it's not done yet, he tells me. I know that's not true. I saw the pages stacked on his desk all nice and neat with "The End" printed on the last page.

What I suspect is it's not because the novel isn't completed that my friend resists sending it out. I think it's because he's a perfectionist, and he can't let it go.

You probably don't need a quiz for this one. Most people who are perfectionists *know* they are. But just in case, look at the following and ask yourself if any of these apply to you:

1. Yes ☐ No ☐ You're very hard on yourself, especially when things go wrong.

2. Yes ☐ No ☐ You spend more time than you should on a task because you want it to be done just right.

3. Yes ☐ No ☐ You have extremely high standards, and will sometimes sacrifice your own well-being to complete a project perfectly.

4. Yes ☐ No ☐ You're the first to find errors and correct them, knowing that finding mistakes in a completed project will drive you nuts.

5. Yes ☐ No ☐ You wait for the "perfect time" to start a new project because you need to feel "ready."

6. Yes ☐ No ☐ You'd like to delegate most tasks, but no one else seems to do them right.

7. Yes ☐ No ☐ Whatever you accomplish, it's never enough. There is always another goal to reach.

8. Yes ☐ No ☐ You tend to ruminate over past mistakes and always vow not to repeat them.

9. Yes ☐ No ☐ If someone isn't pleased with your work, it stresses you out so much that you feel anxious.

10. Yes ☐ No ☐ To ask for help makes you feel weak.

11. Yes ☐ No ☐ If you're not in control of a project, you fear it won't be done right.

12. Yes ☐ No ☐ You put so much of yourself into your work that you risk burnout.

13. Yes ☐ No ☐ You say you'll relax when everything is done, but it's never done.

14. Yes ☐ No ☐ It's hard for you not to double- and triple-check everything. Even small projects must be perfect.

15. Yes ☐ No ☐ You strive for happiness, but your high expectations are impossible to meet, often leaving you down and depressed.

## How Many of These Statements Applied to You?

If you found that four or more of these described you, you tend toward perfectionism. If more than that described you, you may be a full-blown perfectionist. Now before you panic, that's not always a bad thing. It will, however, make it harder for you than it would be for a non-perfectionist to find time to write and to be productive during that time. Here's why:

> **Perfectionists are less productive overall:** They spend too much time trying to get every project just right, which leaves them always running behind.
>
> **Perfectionists procrastinate:** Because they fear failure, they resist starting a project until they feel "ready."
>
> **Perfectionists are always critiquing:** They edit their work as they're writing it, which makes it difficult to get into a rhythm of creative output.

If you're a perfectionist, you may think that the only way you can become more productive is to stop being a perfectionist, but this is usually impossible, and not really necessary. Instead, you need to learn the positive and negative aspects of this trait, and how to get around the negative ones so they don't sabotage your writing time.

## Embrace the Positive Aspects of Perfectionism

Every character trait has both a positive and negative side. Someone who is very detail-oriented, for example, is likely to shine at carrying a project through to a successful conclusion, but may have a hard time seeing the bigger picture, or envisioning the overall end game. A brilliant visionary, on the other hand, is likely to have difficulty attending to everything that needs to be done on a project, and without help, may miss something really important.

Most people can't change these inherent characteristics. Not completely. Studies have shown that basic personality traits tend to stay constant throughout our lifetimes. Paul T. Costa Jr., scientist emeritus at the laboratory of behavioral science at the National Institutes of Health, found in his studies: "It's not that personality is fixed and can't change. But it's relatively stable and consistent. What you see at 35, 40 is what you're going to see at 85, 90."

That means that if you are a perfectionist, it's going to be nearly impossible to *stop* being so. To ask someone to do that is like asking a visionary to become detail-oriented, or the detail- oriented person to suddenly take on the visionary attitude. They can try, but they're likely to end up frustrated, and worse, to lose confidence in their abilities as a whole.

Instead, perfectionists need to embrace the positive aspects of the trait. Ann MacDonald, writing in *Harvard Health*, agrees that perfectionism can be a good thing: "Desirable aspects of this personality trait include conscientiousness, endurance, satisfaction with life, and the ability to cope with adversity. This helps explain why some perfectionists become corporate leaders, skilled surgeons, or Olympic champions."

In fact, there are many ways being a perfectionist will benefit your writing or creative career.

**Perfectionists always try to make their work better.** A perfectionist writer is likely to never be satisfied, and that can be a good thing, because it's a powerful motivator. This writer will probably attend classes, read more, and work to get better at his craft.

**Perfectionists are detail-oriented.** Hyper-organized and hard-working, perfectionists take care of the details and more. They write the books with the accurate facts, and design the websites that rarely miss an important update.

**Perfectionists produce admirable work.** Yes, it may take a perfectionist longer to get her work done, but it's often worth it. The finished prose is a product of beauty and you can feel the care put into crafting every sentence.

**Perfectionists are determined.** They hold high standards for themselves, and are motivated to do what they need to do to get where they want to go. They are able to endure setbacks and keep fighting in pursuit of their goals.

**Perfectionists are good editors.** These writers actually enjoy finding shortcomings in their stories, because it's fun to fix them. They excel at editing not only their own work, but that of other writers, as well, if they choose to offer their editing services.

## The Dark Side of Perfectionism

Unfortunately, perfectionism has a dark side, particularly if you're trying to become more productive and make more time for your writing. It's one of those personality traits that will get in your way over and over again. Here's how:

1. **Everything takes longer:** Because a perfectionist is concerned with getting things just right, she's likely to take longer to do just about any project. She has difficulty finding time to write, because the other things on her to-do list don't get done.

2. **Writer's block is a looming issue:** A perfectionist tends to criticize from the get-go, so it's often difficult for him to get started on a project. He will see the flaws in his idea before he even writes a word. Even if he gets a few paragraphs down, he'll soon be criticizing those, too, which can quickly lead to writer's block. Next time he has a moment to write, he'll look at that file and think about everything that's wrong with it, and often get discouraged and abandon it altogether.

3. **Criticism is hard to take…*really* hard:** A perfectionist writer tends to define herself by her achievements. That makes accepting criticism of her work extremely difficult, because it feels like criticism of *her*, personally. This makes it very hard for her to learn and grow, as she tends to hide her work from others, believing that one day she'll get it perfect, and then no one will be able to criticize.

4. **Burnout is always just around the corner:** If allowed to get out of hand, perfectionism can cause burnout in a hurry. Writers may overwork themselves to make sure *everything* is perfect, from their next novel to their next blog post to their next email, to the point that they eventually buckle under the

demanding load. The result can be exhaustion and depression or even a serious illness.

5. **No accomplishment is ever enough:** Perfectionists find it hard to celebrate their successes. They win an award and figure the competition wasn't that stiff. They get a publishing contract and fret about marketing. They hit the bestseller's list and worry they'll never get there again. It can lead to a downward spiral and an unhappy life.

This side of perfectionism isn't fun. Perfectionists will sometimes freely admit to being unable to forgive themselves for mistakes, constantly finding flaws in their work, and feeling badly in general about their accomplishments or perceived lack of.

These are all negative emotions, and as I've mentioned, negative emotions are not motivating. You need positive ones to compel you to sit down and write.

---

### Time Treasure

## Overcome Negative Perfectionist Tendencies

If you're still not sure if you're a perfectionist, turn back to the questionnaire at the beginning of this chapter and take it again. It's possible that you'll admit to even more tendencies than you did the first time around. That's okay. Now you can embrace the good qualities as well as learn to moderate the bad ones so they don't slow you down.

You need time to write. That means you're going to have

to let some things go, and identify those projects that you can allow to be imperfect. The following tips will help:

- **Everything is not a priority:** Identify projects that don't matter as much, and allow them to be sub-par. Delegate some of the housework at home or the less important tasks at work. Allow one project you do to be just "okay." You'll probably never feel comfortable letting some projects go without being "perfect," but you can get better at it.

- **Realize that your standards are super high:** Most perfectionists have higher standards than others. What seems good to someone else will seem mediocre to you. Realize when this tendency hurts your productivity. Practice doing something well, and then let it go. Stop short of perfect.

- **Focus on productivity, not perfection:** Perfectionists are less productive because they spend too much time on everything, including smaller projects that don't matter much (e.g., proofreading a memo for a third time). Make productivity your goal, and let your perfectionism work on *that* for a while! Give yourself a deadline for every project, and make sure you meet it.

- **When you feel tense, let go:** When the negative traits of perfectionism arise, the body usually responds, too. Muscles tense, becoming stiff and rigid. When this happens, bring your shoulders down, breathe deeply, and

> *allow* the current crisis to unfold naturally so you can deal with it in a productive rather than a perfectionist way.
>
> - **Think of failure as a game:** Perfectionists fear failure. They work to get everything just right so they *don't fail*. To get past this fear, make it a game to see how many mistakes you can commit, not by faking it, but by trying new things more often. Send out *more* submissions and query *more* agents. Experiment with different types of writing. Maybe try poetry, flash fiction, or something in a different genre. Enter your work in *more* contests. Gradually, failure won't seem like such a big deal. You may also surprise yourself at the successes you experience!

## Never Permit Perfectionism to Hijack your Writing Time

Realize that your perfectionism is probably not going to go away, and that's okay. In many ways, it can benefit your career. All you need to do is limit its potential destructiveness by becoming more aware of how it affects your productivity.

Practice the coping techniques and suggestions you learned here. Focus more on turning your perfectionism "on" and "off" as you need it. "On" for priority projects, "off" for everything else.

Most importantly, don't let your perfectionist tendencies erode your writing time. When you're in the middle of a project and notice you're spending too much time on it, ask yourself if it's that important. Remind yourself of your priorities. Choose to let more things go, and enjoy the rewards of your creative time instead.

CHAPTER 16

# SABOTEUR #5—WORKAHOLISM

**W**ORK, WORK, AND more work. Americans work hard, and we're proud of it. That's how it was in my house growing up—I was raised to work hard. My parents believed that "the harder you work, the luckier you get," as my father used to say. I've carried that work ethic into my adult life, and for the most part, it's served me well. Hard work is the key to success in many ways, there's no doubt.

But at some point, my "hard working" character trait got in the way. Rather than realizing I needed to sacrifice some activities to make time to write, I believed I just had to work harder, get it all done faster, and then drive myself to put in more hours on my writing after that. As you can imagine, this didn't work very well.

You may have this trait, too, and not realize how much it can sabotage your productivity on your creative projects. All that time you spend at your day job, working to pay the bills and keep a roof over your head, plus the work you do for your family and friends, say nothing of the volunteering you do for the community or for your church, and then the extra projects you pick up because you feel passionate about them…can cause you to run yourself into the ground.

Meanwhile, you may still feel guilty because you're not getting as much writing done as you'd like to.

Do you think that "working harder" is the answer? For you, it's probably not.

## Determine if You're a Workaholic

There's a fine line between working hard and being a workaholic, so first you need to find out where you fall on the working spectrum. Rate each of the following statements from 1 to 5, with 1 being "not true" and 5 being "definitely true."

1. \_\_\_\_\_ I was raised to work hard.
2. \_\_\_\_\_ I was taught that if you work hard, you can become anything you want to be.
3. \_\_\_\_\_ My work needs to get done first, before anything else.
4. \_\_\_\_\_ I feel unsettled if I have to leave a project undone.
5. \_\_\_\_\_ I feel responsible for doing the work I'm supposed to do.
6. \_\_\_\_\_ I feel like I can't relax or enjoy time off until all the work is done.
7. \_\_\_\_\_ I always have a long "to-do" list and often feel like I'm running behind.
8. \_\_\_\_\_ I put work first and will forego my own needs or well-being to get it done.
9. \_\_\_\_\_ I'd like to find more time to write, but I just have too much work to do.

10. _____ I work harder than most other people in my life.

If your total score is between 30–50, this is an area of concern for you, and you should keep reading. If your score was lower than 30, you're probably not a workaholic, but you may still find some useful information in this chapter about fitting more writing time into your life.

## Working Harder is Not Always the Solution

Hard work is necessary for a successful writing career, but there's a point at which working harder results in diminishing returns. Researchers say that after about fifty hours a week, productivity drops off sharply, and continues to take a nosedive with each additional hour worked. It may be hard to believe, but most people who worked seventy hours produced no more than those who work a mere fifteen hours.

According to a 2014 Gallup poll, most Americans work an average of forty-seven hours a week, while four out of ten work at least fifty. The actual hours may be even higher, since many of us take work home now. Writers tack on even more with the writing they do every day. Even if you enjoy it, writing still requires the same focused attention as work (often more), which adds to your daily workload.

All this extra work takes its toll on productivity. The more hours you work, the less likely you are to get the recommended seven to eight hours of sleep per night that you need. As I explained in Chapter 13, sleep deprivation kills productivity and creativity, resulting in less original thought and output.

What's more, the longer you work, the less effective your brain becomes, especially if you're forty-plus years old. One study reported that after entering your fourth decade, working more than 25 hours a week could cause a negative impact on mental functioning. In any case, no matter what your age now, keep in mind that with each passing year, you'll need more recovery time to keep your brain sharp. Don't expect that you can put in the all-nighters like you did in your twenties and still produce great writing.

Colin McKenzie, economics professor at Keio University in Japan, says that working far too much is worse than not working at all when it comes to cognitive function: "In the beginning work stimulates the brain cells. The stress associated with work physically and psychologically kicks in at some point and that affects the gains you get from working."

This starts a downward spiral—putting in more time at work cuts into your time to sleep, eat right, and exercise, which wears you down to the point that you're chronically tired and irritable with a brain that's not functioning at full capacity.

### Don't be a "Busyness" Addict

If you are a workaholic, or know you're putting in more hours at work than you *really* need to, ask yourself: What's the payoff? For some of us, work is the only place we feel truly in control. Others cling to the office to avoid unpleasantness at home. Many of us, however, are simply addicted to "busyness."

Brigid Schulte, author of *Overwhelmed: Work, Love, and Play When No One Has the Time*, talks about this strange phenomenon: "Somewhere around the end of the 20th century," she writes, "busyness became not just a way of life but a badge of honor. And life, sociologists say, became an exhausting everydayathon."

Researchers have found clues to this cultural trend in—of all things—those holiday letters that people write and send around Christmas time. North Dakota State University professor Ann

Burnett studied decades of them, dating back to 1976. She found that earlier letters talked about the "blessings of the season," while more recent ones talked more about the "frenetic pace of life." The modern-day letters read more like lists of achievements, with terms like "crazy" and "hectic" and phrases like "on the run," and "it's hard to believe it's that time of year again," repeated more often.

It's not that people are complaining. Instead, Burnett notes, they're bragging. Many of us have fallen into the trap of believing that if we're moving fast and achieving, we're relevant. Admitting to taking some time off and relaxing wouldn't look "impressive" or "successful."

This dangerous trend is hurting our physical and emotional health. Andrew Smart, author of *The Art and Science of Doing Nothing*, says excessive busyness is not only bad for the brain, it can have serious health consequences. "In the short term," he writes, "busyness destroys creativity, self-knowledge, emotional well-being, your ability to be social— and it can damage your cardiovascular health."

It's hard to deny—in our society today, busyness is equated with success. Stop and ask yourself what success means to you. If you're not getting your writing done, it's time to see busyness for the addiction it is, and rethink your priorities.

---

Time Treasure

## **Make Writing as Important as Work**

Ask yourself why you like to work so much. If you don't, why are you still doing it? If you're struggling with financial issues, you may have little choice in how many hours you spend at work, but try not to blindly accept that idea. You may be able to get creative with your schedule or downsize enough that you can afford to cut back just a little.

If finances aren't the issue, get real with your feelings. Find out what's really motivating you to cling so tightly to your work. If you tend to always put work first, and feel just a little proud because you're so busy, ask yourself how you're going to feel five or ten years from now if you continue doing what you're doing today.

Obviously you're not getting the time to write that you'd like or you wouldn't be reading this book. If you adhere to your current schedule, it's likely you'll still be frustrated about that five years from now. If that's not acceptable to you, it's time to take some steps to decrease your workload.

One thing that helps is to elevate writing's importance in your life. Yes, work puts money in the bank, food in the cabinets, and a roof over your head, but as long as you don't have time to write, part of you is going to feel incomplete. Worse, you're likely to go through life regretting the decisions you've made.

Try to balance the scales a bit more. Ask yourself if you really need to work fifty-plus hours a week, or if you could cut back and use the hours you gain for writing. What is true in every situation is that time to write will not appear out of thin air—you have to make it, and workaholics most always need to pull it from their work schedules.

CHAPTER 17

# SABOTEUR #6— DESTRUCTIVE GOAL-SETTING

I MENTIONED AT THE beginning of this book that my writing goal was to get a traditional publishing contract. I did all the "right" things you're supposed to do when engaged in goal-setting. I wrote it down. I spoke affirmations about it. ("I'm a traditionally published author.") I acted as if: What would a traditionally published author do?

But for years my goal eluded me, and that was discouraging. Really discouraging. My response wasn't productive. I didn't submit my novel at all for long periods. I felt like I'd failed, even though I'd submitted to only about ten publishers over a period of five years. Rejections made me doubt my ability.

I've heard many variations on this story: Aspiring writers set goals they think will motivate them to succeed, only to discover down the road that the goals actually did the exact opposite. Don't get me wrong. I wholeheartedly believe in goals. They can inspire action, and action is required to make your dreams come true. But some goals do the opposite: They end up inspiring *inaction*.

The issue with my goal? Well, for one thing, it was way too broad—there weren't enough actionable steps. Many writerly goals are like this. Let me show you how not to get stuck in this trap—with the wrong goal—as it can completely destroy your productivity.

## Six Destructive Goals Writers Should Avoid

The six goals we're going to talk about may sound great on the surface, but they will motivate you for only a short time before discouraging you or even leading you to think you're not "good enough" to make it.

Take a close look at these goals and see if any of them could be responsible for your struggle to move forward. Then we'll set new goals that are more likely to boost your productivity and carry you through a lifetime of successful writing.

### 1. I want to be a bestselling novelist.

Unfortunately, it's much harder to do this than most people realize. To reach the *Wall Street Journal's* bestseller list, you need to sell 3,000 copies in the first week after launch. The *New York Times* list takes 9,000 in first week sales.

Yet in 2015, Andrew O'Hagan's *The Illuminations* (Faber & Faber), which was long-listed for the Man Booker prize, had sold less than 3,000 before the announcement of the prize. Tom McCarthy's *Satin Island* (Jonathan Cape) sold less than 1,000 before the announcement. The recognition boosted sales for both, but not as much as you might think—only by a few hundred in each case at the time of the reporting.

The thing is, you can write an awesome, well-reviewed book and still not have a bestseller. That doesn't mean it can't happen. It only means that if you set your future happiness on this goal, you're likely to get discouraged. Then if your first (or second or third) book doesn't make it, suddenly you're thinking, "Who am I fooling? This is never going to happen. Why am I wasting my time?" This thinking is dangerous because it convinces you that your writing time has been in vain.

**2. I'd like to make enough money writing to quit my day job.**

Writers who achieve this are in the minority. In 2015, the Author's Guild (a group that supports published writers and their rights) conducted a member survey to determine how much money writers actually earned. They then compared the data to that gathered from a previous survey conducted in 2009.

The results were not encouraging. Full-time authors saw a decrease of thirty percent in their yearly income, while part-time authors saw a thirty-eight percent decrease. Only a little over a third—thirty-nine percent—supported themselves on writing alone. Most still worked supporting jobs.

Publishing is a fast-changing industry, and is likely to have changed again by the time you read this. Of course, you can make money writing, particularly if you write fast and can produce a large number of books in a short period of time. Some writers also teach, give speeches, conduct workshops, or combine traditional and self-publishing to make ends meet.

Even if you do manage to get published, it's difficult to make enough money to support yourself *and* your writing habit. One of the reasons is that authors are more responsible than ever for marketing their own work. Publishers are concerned about the bottom line, and are most likely to put marketing dollars behind bestselling authors or celebrities, which leaves the rest of us to shoulder the burden of marketing ourselves, and have no doubt—it takes money.

Here's a partial list of what writers usually end up paying for:

- Hosting fees for a website (strongly recommended vs. free blogging platforms)
- Image fees
- Design fees
- Photography (if you want to have a quality headshot, and for quality blog posts)
- Contest submissions
- Writer's conferences
- Book blog tours
- Book trailers
- Book giveaways
- Travel to bookstores
- Apps and software
- Membership fees (to writers' groups)
- Books and courses (for your own education)
- Any advertising or book promotion
- Editing and proofreading (if you're self-publishing, and often even if you're traditionally publishing but want to improve your work before submitting)
- Writing equipment (computers, printers, tablets, scanners, etc.)
- Research costs

Yes, you can save money along the way by making economical choices or choosing free or do-it-yourself options, but you're still going to need some money to get your name out there.

Most people tend to get stressed out if they don't have enough money to pay the rent and groceries. If after five years (or longer) you're finding you still have to do other work besides your writing (which most writers do), you could get really discouraged if this is your main goal.

**3. I dream of winning the _____ prize.**

Again, this may sound like a goal that would encourage your writing, but let's take a closer look. You can write a great book and submit it to contests, but the competition is always stiff, and what happens if your book doesn't place? You often cannot try again the next year, because most prizes are awarded to books in their year of publication.

There are contests you can enter prior to publication that will still allow you to enter again the next year as long as you weren't selected as a finalist, but it's still tough competition. If you're counting on eventually placing, you're likely to get discouraged. That makes this a destructive goal. You're putting your future in someone else's hands. The judges shouldn't have that much power over your creative life.

**4. I want to get an awesome agent.**

You may dream of saying, "My agent loves my story. She's submitting it to Random House this week." Meanwhile, you imagine outrageous advances and bestseller lists.

Except this rarely happens, particularly for first-time authors.

The reality is that it's just as hard (some say harder) to find a good agent as it is to find a publisher. It can take months if not years of your time submitting and attending writer's conferences and looking for that perfect match.

Once you have an agent, that's no guarantee your book will be published. He may submit your book to several publishers, but be unable to sell it. Or, if he does, it could be to a small, indie publisher you could have queried yourself, but instead you end up paying fifteen percent in perpetuity because the agent submitted it instead.

Yes, it can happen. First-time authors have found perfect agents and gone on to get good publishing contracts. But there's no guarantee. There's nothing wrong with trying, but it can be a discouraging process if this is your main goal.

## 5. I dream of getting published by one of the big five.

Penguin Random House, Harper Collins, Simon & Schuster, Hachette, Macmillan: they're called the "big 5" because after years of consolidations and shutdowns, they're the biggest remaining commercial publishers. Most of us grew up knowing these names, and are aware of the prestige that goes along with being published by any of them.

Deals with these guys have gotten more difficult to obtain over the past couple decades, though. Some would say near impossible, especially for new authors (though it can happen), and nearly impossible without an established agent.

You can put years into a book and have a perfectly fine story, but if your goal all along was to have it accepted by one of these heavy hitters and it's not, it's going to feel like you wasted your time.

That would be sad, as there are plenty of high-quality independent publishers and small presses that can give a new author a really good start. There's no reason to limit yourself to such a narrow possibility. Some of today's most famous authors started at small presses.

## 6. I dream of handing my family/friends/loved ones a copy of my book.

I know a lot of authors who were motivated by the idea of, "I'll show them!" It works until you publish that first book and hold it up proudly for everyone to see and they…don't really give a darn.

People have busy lives. They're running around doing their thing, and don't have time to make you feel like you've finally arrived. Don't be surprised if some (or all) of your family members never read your book. It happens all the time. Your friends may congratulate you. They may even buy a copy but then not read it, or fail to leave you a review.

For writers, publishing a book is the ultimate dream, but for others, well, it's nice but not that big a deal. If people didn't respect you before, they're unlikely to change their minds because you published a book.

That's okay. It keeps writers grounded. It reminds us that there are a lot of other things in life besides writing and publishing. But setting a goal based solely on impressing others is doomed from the start, as you can't control what other people think.

## Don't Give Up Your Power to Destructive Goals

The one big thing that's wrong with all these goals is that to achieve them, you must rely on factors *outside of your control.* You cannot control what contest judges think of your story, or what an agent or editor thinks, or even what your mom thinks.

When you base your success as a writer on what other people deem worthy, you're totally giving your power away. That's deadly for a creative individual. You *need* that power. You have to consistently motivate and encourage yourself, and often it's not easy. There are so many things that can discourage you along the way.

That's why you need achievable goals that help build your self-esteem and confidence. It's fun to dream, and there's nothing wrong with *wanting* to be a bestseller, *wanting* to get an agent, *wanting* to place in a contest, or *wanting* to sell a lot of books so you can quit your day job. Nothing at all wrong with wanting these things. Just don't use them to set your yearly goals.

Set only the goals that *empower you*, goals you can achieve without help from anyone else. Working toward these types of goals will keep you inspired day after day, month after month. You may get discouraged along the way, but you'll be able to handle it because you're in the driver's seat and remain in control of your future.

## Set Productive Goals that Inspire Action

A productive goal is a goal that inspires measureable action over the long-term. If your goals don't do that, they're not worthwhile goals. Fortunately, setting productive goals is easy when you test each one against these three criteria:

1. Is this goal totally within your power to achieve?
2. Does this goal inspire you to take concrete action toward your writing dreams?
3. Does this goal keep you accountable?

Here's how it works. Say your goal is to write a new novel by the end of the year, and you're starting in January. Check it against the criteria above. First, it is completely within your control to achieve this goal, so you're good on number one. But on number two, it's a little shaky. It may inspire you to take action for the first few weeks, but when the writing gets difficult (as it always does in the middle of a novel), you'll get discouraged. You may think, "Well, I've got a lot of time. I'll write tomorrow." And tomorrow, and tomorrow, until you get to December and your novel remains unfinished. So on number two, yes, it inspired you to take concrete action, but not for very long.

This brings us to number three: This goal doesn't keep you accountable in an efficient way. You've got an entire year to finish the novel, but you could procrastinate or get discouraged and stop working on it consistently. The only check-in time is at the end of the year, which leaves way too much room for slacking off. So on #3, it just doesn't work at all.

In this case, the better goal would be to write a novel in one year by writing 1,750 words a week, or 250 words a day. If you stick to this goal, you'll have about 90,000 words at the end of the year—certainly enough to make up a novel. This restated goal meets all three of our criteria. Achieving it is entirely in your hands, it's simple enough that it will inspire you to take action, and it holds you accountable. If you fall behind, you'll know right away and you'll be motivated to catch up.

You can apply these three criteria to almost any goal you want to accomplish. If you want to make more money with your books, for example, instead of saying, "I want to make $25,000 a year with my books next year," you might set a goal to take four key action steps toward becoming a more profitable author:

1. take one online marketing workshop every other month,

2. read one book per month about making money publishing and take good notes that you can use in your own business,

3. spend at least an hour a week on marketing research,

4. and try at least three new marketing campaigns over the course of the year.

All of these actions are completely within your power, and with definitive deadlines, they will keep you accountable. It's possible that by the end of the year you may not have $25,000 in the bank from your writing, but you will have significantly increased your odds of knowing *how* to make more money. If you keep at it, you're much more likely to get what you want than if you simply set an arbitrary income level as your goal.

## Set Goals Related to Your "Wants"

The key is to start with what you want (to make money), and use that want to set an achievable goal (e.g., to conduct three giveaways, two blog tours, and ten book signings by the end of the year.)

If you want to place in a contest, for example, set a goal to submit to ten of them this year—one per month except for December and August. Narrow it down even more and decide to research contests for one hour each week in preparation for your once-a-month submission. Add some activities that will get you feedback on your work, like hiring a book editor, taking advantage of writing critiques at conferences, or working with another writing mentor. Narrow it down by deciding to get eight critiques on your work this year, four by June and the other four by October.

If you come to the end of the year and you submitted to only four contests instead of ten, you didn't reach your goal. If you submitted to all ten, no matter what the outcome, you reached your goal and you can feel proud of that. In addition, you will have learned a lot more about submitting to contests, which of course will increase your odds of placing in the future.

If you want to get an agent, set a goal to submit to twenty of them this year, and to meet with at least three in person at writer's conferences or other events. Follow a similar pattern to narrow down the process so you're researching agents every week and submitting every month. Make your goal one that inspires regular and measurable action.

---

### Time Treasure
## Set an Actionable Goal

Let's set a goal for increasing your writing time right now. Fill in the blank:

I commit to writing _____ words per _____ (day/week).

That's it. Doesn't have to be fancy. You can make a commitment as big or as small as you want, but I suggest starting small, as small actions lead to bigger ones. If you go too big, you risk feeling overwhelmed, which can discourage you from even getting started.

If you've already got a daily writing goal in place, set a second goal. Maybe you want to get better at plot, characterization, or setting. Decide how you're going to do that (courses, books, editing, etc.). Or maybe you've already got a book out there, and you need to set a marketing goal.

Test your goal against the three criteria above, and then write it down here (use your own notebook if you need more space):

I commit to _____(task)
by _____ (deadline).

Take action on your new goal today. Good luck!

CHAPTER 18

# SABOTEUR #7—BELIEF

If you think this chapter is about believing in yourself, you're right, but probably not in the way you think. Depending on how you go about it, trying to "believe" in your talent or creative abilities may help or hurt your motivation for your creative work.

We're often told we have only to believe in ourselves to make our dreams come true, but that's easier said than done. It's difficult to manifest belief out of thin air. Plus, the idea that all you have to do is believe and everything will fall in place is a myth. It just doesn't work that way. Achieving anything of value requires time, practice, commitment, and effort, as well as the ability to master certain skills along the way.

On the other hand, if you lack belief in yourself, it's going to be a hard road for you. If you don't feel like you *can* do this, every time you get a moment to write, your lack of confidence will sabotage that time.

Imagine you sit down with your computer or notebook, but in the back of your head, you don't believe you have what it takes to be a writer, complete your new project, sell your new book—whatever it is. That lack of belief is likely to lead you to procrastinate. You may suddenly decide you need some coffee. Once the coffee is brewed you may decide you've got to pick up the living room, rearrange your desk, feed the cat…you know how it goes. Soon your writing time is gone and you've got nothing to show for it.

This is how a lack of belief in your abilities can sabotage your writing time and productivity.

Creating an authentic feeling of true belief in yourself, however, is more complicated than you may think. If I told you at this moment to "believe in yourself," you wouldn't magically believe you could write a bestseller. So let's talk seriously about belief, and what it really takes.

## Focus on Achievement Rather Than Belief

When I was getting my bachelor's degree, I took some education classes. At that time, the instructors were all about boosting students' self-esteem. This was the era that spawned such activities as giving trophies to everyone on the team just for participation, holding ceremonies where every child received an award regardless of performance, and complimenting kids all day long whether they deserved it or not.

Within about a decade, research showed that this unearned praise didn't help kids at all. Even those with high self-esteem weren't necessarily performing better than those with lower self-esteem. U.S. eighth-graders, for example, had high levels of confidence in their math abilities—much higher than their counterparts in other countries, like Singapore—yet had only middling performance levels (lower than Singapore students) on an international math exam, according to a Brown Center Report on Education.

The same thing happened in the adult world, but in a slightly different way. Jumping on the "self-esteem" bandwagon, personal growth gurus started telling adults to heap empty praise on themselves—through affirmations. Affirmations have been big for a while now. The idea is that if you repeat to yourself some sort of affirming statement, such as, "I'm a great writer" or "I'm extremely talented"—even if there is no evidence to support the fact—over time, that statement will magically come true.

Unfortunately, the opposite often happens. Current research shows that spouting positive affirmations about yourself that you don't really believe can actually make you feel *worse*, not better.

I tried affirmations for a while. I wrote them out on sticky notes and posted them around the house. I told myself I was a traditionally published novelist. I repeated statements like, "I've written a great novel" and "I'm thrilled with my publishing contract." I'm here to tell you—affirmations don't work. Every time I said those statements, another part of me echoed something like, "That's not true," or "Yeah, right." I could feel it inside, and even though I tried to ignore that feeling, it wouldn't go away.

What does work is actually *achieving what you want to achieve*. Science now suggests that only when you do something well, will you truly believe that you can do it well again. It seems like a "chicken or the egg" conundrum, but the truth is that the more you succeed at something, the more likely you are to believe you can continue to succeed in that area.

If you're a runner, for example, and you win a race, you're more likely to believe you can win another one. Prior to winning that first race, however, your belief might be shaky, and telling yourself you're the fastest runner in the group probably won't help much, especially if you're not sure you are. The truth is you just don't know you can do something until you've actually done it.

What you have to do is start small. Find something you can truly believe in, and use that to authentically motivate and inspire yourself. We'll talk about how you can do that in a moment.

## Forget About "Talent"

Before we go into how you can use your belief to your advantage, we have to address this issue of talent. Throughout the years, you've probably asked yourself and various other people in your life if you have the talent to be a good writer. We all have, but unfortunately, no one is qualified to answer that question—not your teacher, editor, friends, or loved ones, and certainly not the workshop leader who tore your story to shreds.

Seeking validation from others is a worthless enterprise. Yes, you will have people praise your writing along the way, but you'll also have people who tell you it's no good. Basing your belief in your own talent on statements given by others is a mistake. It will only send you on an emotional roller coaster.

Humans have far too much potential to learn to ever be categorized as not having enough talent. There's no way to accurately measure talent in the creative world, anyway. So let's just set aside the question. Believing yourself to be a great writer is *not* necessary for you to become a great writer.

That's good news. Though there are writing prodigies out there—and you may be one of them—most writers have to put in years of practice before they develop the storytelling skills they need to produce publishable work. During that time, it's perfectly natural to doubt your own talent, ability, and even your purpose as a writer.

Let me say that again: *It's perfectly normal to doubt your own talent, ability, and even your purpose as a writer.*

When it happens, don't sweat it. When you feel that lack of belief inside you, resist telling yourself empty affirmations like "I'm a great writer!" or "I have a lot of creative talent!" It won't help you, and may even hurt you. Instead, decide to believe in something much smaller and more realistic.

## Shrink Your Beliefs

If you want to succeed at your writing goals, including the goal of becoming more productive, you need to believe in yourself, but that belief needs to feel authentic. Unless you've won the Pulitzer Prize, you're probably going to find it difficult to truly believe that you're a Pulitzer-Prize-worthy author. You can, however, believe in your ability to find more time to write.

Ask yourself right now: Am I capable of making time in my schedule to write? I can't think of anyone who can't answer that question in the affirmative. Even if you're the busiest person on the planet, you can find fifteen minutes in your day to write.

What's magical about this sort of belief is that it can lead to other, bigger beliefs down the road. Remember that the more you achieve, the more you will *believe* you can achieve.

Let's say you believe you can find time to write. Because of that belief, you open up a half-hour in your daily schedule. Within a week you'll have amassed several pages of work. You will have succeeded at your goal, which will lead you to believe that you can succeed again.

The next week you'll continue to find time to write, and maybe this time you'll get in an hour a day instead of thirty minutes. At the end of that week, you will have a higher level of confidence in your ability to write regularly. As long as you continue down this road, your belief will grow, as will your writing skill, simply because you're putting in the time to practice.

Before long, you'll be believing in your ability to submit your novel to an agent or editor, and then believing in your ability to keep improving your craft, and then believing in your ability to learn how to market your book. The trick is to believe in something that makes sense to you. You *can* learn new things. You *can* practice. You *can* take more frequent actions to support your writing aspirations. You don't have to bother trying to convince yourself that you're the next Margaret Atwood or Dennis Lehane. You don't need to be. You're called to write (or to create). Trust in that, and in your ability to take small steps that stay true to that calling.

**Authentically Build Your Beliefs**

The cool thing about belief is that it's easy to build. It's like using Legos to create a castle. If you don't yet believe—truly believe—that you can be a great writer, all you have to do is shrink your beliefs. In this case, you took the belief of being a great writer and shrank it down to one of its smallest elements—believing you can make time in your schedule to write.

As you progress in your career, you will grow that belief to one that applies to your ability to publish your books, market them well, run a popular blog, or build a reputable author platform. Belief in your ability to improve, as long as it's authentic, may be the only belief that you truly need to succeed.

Jo Boaler, Stanford Professor of Mathematics Education and author of *Mathematical Mindsets*, found that students with "growth mindsets" who believed that if they worked hard they could learn difficult concepts, consistently outperformed students with "fixed mindsets" who believed they couldn't change their basic level of intelligence.

You don't have to force unrealistic beliefs upon yourself. You don't have to believe at this moment that you're going to be a bestselling writer to start making progress toward that dream. The more you write, get feedback, learn, practice, and write some more, the more your belief will grow, naturally. No affirmations required.

In other words, don't let your belief that you have to "believe" sabotage your writing time. If you're not sure you've got what it takes right now, welcome to the club. Most writers and other creative artists frequently feel that way. Instead, break it down. Let your belief work for you at a more authentic level. Allow a small belief to be the seed from which the eventual "I'm a great writer" belief will emerge.

---

**Time Treasure**

## Start Believing

Ask yourself this question: What can I believe about myself at this very moment that will help me fulfill my writing goals? Some examples may include:

- I believe I can make time in my schedule to write fifteen minutes a day.
- I believe I can find a way to write 250 words a week.
- I believe I can write a story, even if it isn't very good.
- I believe I can improve my writing skills.
- I believe I can learn to market my books.
- I believe I can learn how to build my author platform.

- I believe I can learn how to set up my own website.
- I believe I can find an editor to help me become a better writer.
- I believe I can submit my story to ten journals this year.

Think about the next step you want to take in your writing career. Maybe you want to publish a novel, but you're having a hard time believing you're "good enough." That's okay—you don't have to believe that you are. You can shrink it down and believe, for example, that you can complete a novel-length manuscript. At this point, completing it is all that is necessary.

Take a moment to write down your new belief below. Make sure you actually believe it, and that it resonates as true within you. Try, too, to find a belief that will help you to move forward in your writing career. If you have already committed to a regular writing practice, for example, don't use that as your belief. Stretch yourself a bit, and think about what's next, such as believing you can submit your finished novel to publishers, or that you can learn the steps you'd need to complete to self-publish it.

I believe:

_____

_____

# PART IV

# FAIL AND TRY AGAIN

**W**ELCOME TO THE last section of the book. Whatever your situation, I hope the information you've read so far will help you apply new ideas to your lifestyle so you can feel like you're making better progress toward your goals. But beware, nothing works overnight. If something I've suggested doesn't work for you right away, don't stop trying. As a creative person, there's one thing you must always be willing to do, and that's *fail, and try again*.

We like it when things are easy. When getting the car repaired, for instance, we expect the mechanic will fix or replace the faulty part so we can be on our way without having to worry about it again. But if after paying the bill the car still doesn't work right, we may get a little irritated and never go back to that mechanic again. Sometimes that's best, because maybe the mechanic wasn't very skilled, but sometimes, it just takes a while to find the real problem, and even a skilled professional requires a little trial and error.

Before you picked up this book, you may have searched for other solutions to your writing time challenges, implemented them, and then when they didn't work, gave up on the dream.

I hope you won't do that this time.

It's the nature of the creative life to continually face new challenges that threaten to slow you down or stop you altogether. Even when you develop new skills to tackle these challenges, it can take several tries before you become truly comfortable with what works best for you. That's why this section is about four final things you must do to continue to be successful at finding time to write:

1. Use your motivation style
2. Be flexible and persistent
3. Find writer solutions
4. Get *grit*

If you can get better at these four things, you'll be able to overcome just about any difficulty and still find time to write and enjoy your creative work. Let's get started.

CHAPTER 19

# USE YOUR MOTIVATION STYLE

I LOVE IT WHEN I meet an aspiring writer at a workshop or conference, and then a few years later see her book show up for sale or as a winning entry in a literary contest. It always makes me stop and smile, realizing that I met one more person who beat the odds, hung in there, and made her dreams come true.

I've known some other amazing writers in my life that unfortunately, no one else will ever hear about. Few will read their stories, and fewer still will ever know about their writing talents, because of one reason: they weren't motivated enough to see it through.

Simply wanting something is not enough, and this includes wanting to be a writer. No matter how much you want to fit writing into your life, how productive you become, how much you change your schedule, or how well you overcome demons like self-doubt and perfectionism, if you're not sufficiently motivated to write on a regular basis, you won't succeed.

Without true motivation, there will be no change in your life, no matter how much you want it—that's just the way it is. Change is hard and we human beings are built to maintain the status quo. We all know this to be true.

Just think about how you feel once you have a schedule set and are finally content with a certain way of life. Everything comes together to maintain that lifestyle, no matter what. In order to bust out of that mold you must hunger for change. You must be so fed up with your current situation that you welcome the obstacles you will encounter, because you know once you get past them, things will get better.

How motivated are you to make changes in your life to support your creativity? Let's find out.

## Quiz: Are You Motivated?

If you have the tiniest bit of doubt as to whether or not you're up for the changes you know you need to make to reach your writing goals, answering these questions should help.

1. A year from now, if you are in the same place as far as your writing is concerned, how will you feel?
    a. That would be the worst ever.
    b. Badly, but I won't beat myself up.
    c. Not great, but writing isn't everything.
    d. Fine. I want to write, but my life is really busy right now.

2. How many writing-related changes have you made since you started reading this book? Don't forget to count scheduling writing time, adopting a new productivity technique, or working on exorcising demons, like self-doubt. Or perhaps your changes were more along the lines of setting up a dedicated writing space, sacrificing an activity to write, etc.
    a. Five or more changes
    b. Three to five changes
    c. One to three changes

d. None

3. How many words have you written in the last week?

    a. 4,000 or more

    b. 2,500–4,000

    c. 500–2,500

    d. None

4. Do you feel you are able take charge of your life and work on your craft to become a better writer?

    a. I feel excited and ready to get to work.

    b. I'm excited, but worried about my ability to make it happen.

    c. I think it's interesting, but I'm not convinced I can make these types of changes in my life.

    d. I'm doubtful that I can fit writing into my current schedule.

5. What is your perception of your creativity since you started reading this book?

    a. I feel like I've been neglecting it and I'm now committed to honoring my unique nature.

    b. I see that it's up to me to nurture my creativity and I hope I can do it.

    c. I'd love to focus more on my creativity, but it's difficult for me.

    d. I like that I'm a creative person, but I can't afford to focus on it at this time in my life.

Total the number of A, B, C, and D answers you had. Mostly

"A" answers mean you're very motivated about finding more time to write. If your answers were mostly in the B and C range, you may be motivated, but not enough to really make this happen right now. Take a minute to ask yourself why you doubt your ability to change. Perhaps you're trying to do too much at once, and setting smaller, more achievable goals will help you to continue moving forward.

If you had mostly "D" answers, your motivation is really lacking and you need to ask yourself if writing is for you. If you still feel compelled to write, take some time to examine your life and your feelings to find out what is standing in your way. Review Chapters 12-18 to see if one of the seven saboteurs is secretly stalling your progress toward your dreams.

Whatever your reasons may be for not being able to find sufficient motivation to change, before you get frustrated and fail, consider first that:

> Everything in your life is a reflection of who you are, and you alone are responsible.

### It's Your Life

When I first came across the statement above years ago, it stopped me dead in my tracks. *You mean, I can't blame the struggles in my life on anyone else?* Certainly it was because of the economy that I wasn't making as much money as I wanted to, or because of the market that I hadn't published a novel, or because of the cold weather that I'd gained a few pounds, or because I was so busy that I hadn't gotten as far as I'd wanted to in my writing career.

It's amazing, really, how much we can play the victim in our own lives. You've likely suffered hardships. Everyone does, but ultimately, you are in charge, unless you give that power away. If you do, that too, is your choice. It all ends at your door.

This struck me as a difficult pill to swallow because at the time, there were definitely things about my life I didn't like. Realizing that those things were there entirely because of me and the choices I'd made was tough. I went a few rounds with self-recrimination before realizing we all make mistakes and there are always things we want to change. The point is that nothing is going to change on its own.

Only you have the power to make things different in your life. Even small changes can lead to repercussions that have a profound effect on your future, and it all starts by being motivated enough to take that first step.

## Three Powerful Motivators

Humans are motivated by three main things:

1. Power
2. People
3. Achievement

In his book *Getting Unstuck: A Guide to Discovering Your Next Career Path*, Timothy Butler states: "Over the years in my work as a psychotherapist, researcher, and career counselor, I have come to appreciate the central role that three social needs (or social 'motivators') play in our life decisions: the need to act in our immediate world, the need to belong, and the need to achieve. A shorthand to expression of these three needs is: power, people, and achievement."

Butler's findings also apply to us writers and our careers. Today, simply writing a book may not be enough for writers wanting to craft their entire living from their work. Tapping into your personal motivation style can help you to not only overcome daily obstacles to get your writing done, but to see more clearly how you might broaden your goals and increase job satisfaction.

Most people are motivated by all three of these needs at one time or another, but usually one tends to stick out a bit more than the other two as being important to you. That one is also more likely to drive most of your decisions. Below are brief descriptions of the three categories. Read them over, and then decide which one sounds like the dominant one for you.

**1. Power**

Those motivated by power find it easy to act in the outside world and go after what they want. They like positions of authority. They want to be players and decision makers, and are often the ones who take charge in groups or lead dinnertime conversations. They volunteer for leadership roles, and enjoy influencing others.

Ask yourself the following questions to find out if power is a strong motivator for you:

- Did you often seek out positions of power? School officer, club president, team captain?

- When you think of your future, do you want to be in charge of something, or leading something?

- Do you think of yourself as managing events, and making decisions?

Though we all have a need for power, some of us define ourselves mostly by our desire for dominance and/or authority and feel out of sync unless we are in charge of something.

## 2. People

Those motivated by people need to belong. Though everyone needs satisfying relationships for optimal physical and mental health, those who find this motivator dominant don't feel "whole" if they aren't involved in relationships that nourish them. They value connection above all else, and seek out roles that offer interpersonal contact. They are definite team players, and have many friends and acquaintances.

This person is comfortable in the role of coach, counselor, teacher, and homemaker. He places high priority on spending time with family and friends, and will likely trade other things in life (like power and achievement) for good relationships.

Ask yourself the following questions to determine if your relationships are powerful motivators for you:

- In your past, were you the one getting friends together? When you were alone, did you feel sort of unsettled and crave interaction?
- Were you the one who worried when arguments and strife entered your social circle?
- Are you someone others lean on when they need help?

## 3. Achievement

Those motivated by achievement have a deep personal need to accomplish their goals, regardless of what that means in terms of relationships or their positions in an organization.

These are the scientists laboring over research for years in the hopes of making a discovery, and the musicians practicing for hours in the basement in the hopes of becoming proficient at a piece. They are looking to achieve their "personal best," and then to raise the bar a little higher. They may be competitive, seeking to outdo others to satisfy their own need for achievement. They enjoy being challenged, and become quickly bored if they're not learning new things. They love to be seen as experts, but don't need to be in charge.

Ask yourself the following questions to see if achievement is a powerful motivator for you:

- In your past, were you the one trying to better your running time, achieve straight As, or become the go-to expert on car engines?
- Are you satisfied only when you win that award you're going after, or when someone in authority recognizes your hard work?
- Do you find jobs that fail to challenge you boring?

## Help in Determining Your Motivation Style

By now you should have a pretty good idea which of the three motivators is most powerful for you. You will likely feel an intuitive knowing or recognition when you read the description that most closely matches your motivation style. If you're still not sure, though, or if you're waffling between a couple, the following exercise may help.

Think back on the big moments in your life. Which ones do you remember as being particularly meaningful? Examples may include the day you won a big contest, or when you were elected as a leader of a group, or when you made a meaningful connection with another person. Write down the five moments that come to mind in the spaces below:

1. _____
2. _____
3. _____
4. _____
5. _____

Now review your list and try to connect the events to one of the three motivating categories above. If your big moments involved people, for instance—when you met your best friend, when your child was born, or when you successfully organized a social activity—you may be people oriented. If they involved positions of authority, such as when you became Vice President in your company, or when you were appointed to lead a certain group or team, you may be motivated by power. If they involved awards or other types of recognition, you may be motivated by achievement.

Once you've identified your primary motivator, it's time to apply that to your writing time, your goals, and your career as a whole. Sit down with a journal or a computer and do some brainstorming on how you can use your motivation style to inspire yourself to take action. With a little reflection, you're likely to come up with your own best answers, but here are a few thoughts to get you started.

## Tap Into Your Desire for Power

If your primary motivator is power, you love to run things. You may be happier self-publishing than traditionally publishing your book so you can control every aspect of the process. You may enjoy writing books or articles that help persuade people to think as you do, or that position you as a leader. You may even want to start an online magazine in your chosen subject area so you can start influencing people right away.

Your writing may support your efforts to gain a higher position in your chosen occupation, or may serve as a vehicle to launch a new company. You may need to feel effective and like you're making an impact, so choose writing topics that support that goal.

Tap into your passions and write to influence people. If you're struggling to make yourself write today, think about whom you may affect if you get that writing done. Beware of one thing—you may enjoy "having written" over writing, so if you find yourself putting off the actual work, dive into a powerful or emotionally arousing scene to get yourself going. Emotional scenes influence people, so you're likely to enjoy those best.

You may also want to pre-publish parts of your work now so you can enjoy readers' reactions. Use your blog for this, guest post on other blogs, or submit pieces of your work to journals, your local newspaper, or other potential outlets like WattPad.

Another good way to motivate yourself is to tell others about your goals. The fact that they might ask you about your progress later on will motivate you to get the work done. Offer to make a presentation that relates to your work, and have beta readers who are willing to look at your early pieces and give you motivating feedback.

## Tap Into Your Desire for Connection

If people are your primary motivator, you love to connect, so use that to your advantage. You may enjoy starting a writer's group, running classes at the library, or setting up some sort of club, like one that focuses on your particular genre. Online coaching may be perfect for you, allowing you to reach a larger number of people and to use your writing skills to help improve their lives. Your writing may lead you to teaching positions, or mentoring.

Perhaps you would like to organize a regular writing retreat. I know some writers who find this really rewarding, as the interaction with other writers is super motivating for them. Once a retreat is established, you can also pull in successful and influential writers, which could open up opportunities you wouldn't have had otherwise.

You may want to write a book about relationships. If your novel is stalling, insert more relationship drama into it. A people person is unlikely to stay interested in a story that doesn't have a good amount of human interaction.

Since you like working with others, co-authoring a book might be right up your alley, or joining with others to start a new cooperative blog. Imagine how you can help others with your writing—maybe self-help is your category—and find supportive friends who provide reassurance and will be there to take you through periods of rejection and challenge. (This is really important for people writers—you need positive support!)

Attend workshops, and when you're alone with your writing, imagine a friendly reader enjoying your work. Better yet, write in a café or somewhere you can enjoy the feeling of other people being around.

## Tap Into Your Desire for Achievement

If achievement is your primary motivator, you need to constantly challenge yourself. Start out by setting deadlines, and put that calendar somewhere you can see it every day, so you can chart your progress. Set goals for yourself, and cross them off as you complete them, so you can feel that sense of accomplishment.

If you get bored with what you're doing, find out how you can set the bar higher. Allow yourself to work toward placing in a contest or getting your work published, or if you've already been published, focus on sales. If you've won an award for your short stories, maybe it's time to see if you could get a book of them published. If you've been published but have yet to see high sales, challenge yourself to become a better marketer or to improve your personal brand.

Seek out opportunities to enter contests that provide critiques. Simple praise doesn't work for you. Find a writing mentor who will challenge you to get better. Take classes that will help you improve your craft, and practice with setting, character, and dialogue.

Don't divide your energies with group activities. They are more likely to distract you than help you. Give yourself time to work alone. Don't be afraid to take risks in your pursuit of achievement. If you're self-publishing, you'll want your book to be the best it can be, so understand the time and commitment that will require. If you're seeking to traditionally publish and you're not succeeding, find out why. Read books, attend conferences, and work on improving your writing. Achievers are great problem-solvers.

Don't forget to celebrate each of your successes, however—achievers are rarely satisfied, which can lead to depression, so take a moment now and then to see how far you've come. Keep track of every milestone so you can look back and remind yourself of all you've accomplished.

Time Treasure:

## Use Your Motivation Style in Your Writing

Knowing your motivation style can help you get more excited about your writing, which will naturally lead you to find more time to work on it. Using what you've learned in this chapter, fill in the blanks below:

Right now, I'm working on _____.
(Examples: A book about dragons, my new website, a short story about a little boy, a potential weekly "slice-of-life" column, etc.)

My main motivation style is _____
(people, power, achievement).

My motivation style is reflected in my current work in the following ways. (If your style is people, for example, maybe you're focusing on a relationship in your current work, you're writing daily in a café or other public place, or you're working on your story with your writers' group. If your style is achievement, maybe you have a future contest deadline on the calendar, you're focusing on improving your character development, or you're working with a new editor or mentor who will take you to the next level. If your style is power, maybe you're working on a non-fiction book or new blog that you hope will influence people in your chosen field. Make the connections where you see them, and if you don't see them, make note of that.)

1. _____

2. _____

3. _____

I could tap into my motivation more by doing the following. (Examples for achievement—research publishers to send my novel to, or set more aggressive deadlines; people—put together a reading group in my genre or plan to attend a writers' conference where I can get a critique; power—invite interested friends over for dinner to discuss the topic in my book or blog, or invite guest bloggers to contribute to my site.)

- Connection 1: _____
- Connection 2: _____
- Connection 3: _____

As you go about your day tomorrow, keep thinking about your style and how it influences you in your daily life. As your awareness increases, you'll start to get more ideas for how to motivate yourself, and you'll become clearer on what types of activities don't work for you.

Consider, too, that you can work on more than one thing at a time. If you're writing a novel, for example, but you find your motivation waning, use your style to start a second project, such as an online magazine, writer's retreat, or even just a different type of story. The important thing is to keep moving forward. Let your inspiration take you in the right direction…for *you*.

CHAPTER 20

# BE FLEXIBLE AND PERSISTENT

LIFE HAS A way of making a mess of our routines. Sometimes it's health problems that get in the way. Other times it's family stresses, job changes, moving, relationship issues, or financial strain. Suddenly those quiet mornings you had so carefully blocked off to write may be filled taking care of an elderly parent or sick child. Afternoons of writing in the car after work may have to be dropped because you have appointments with a therapist or have to rush to a new job interview.

Other times, it's less traumatic changes that reveal your treasured routine isn't going to work anymore. You may take on a new venture that keeps you up late at night, stealing the writing time you used to have before bed. Your boss may implement lunchtime meetings so you can no longer use that time to create. Or you may simply go through a life change that has you feeling more energetic at night, when you used to be rearing to go in the morning.

We all deal with these things as best we can, but to enjoy a long-term creative career, you'll want to become flexible in your approach to time management. Yes, there are occasions when you must persist and keep to your writing schedule, but there are other times when you'll need to allow for the intrusions of life's unexpected. It's an interesting combination you must develop: the ability to be flexible, and at the same time, the ability to know when stubborn persistence is required.

### When to Choose One or the Other

It can be confusing to determine whether persistence or flexibility is needed in a given situation, but examining your feelings and your circumstances will help guide you toward the right action. Here are some examples:

You probably need to be flexible if…

- you're not getting your writing done because something important is interfering with your writing time, and
- you're starting to get frustrated and overwhelmed about it.

Find out exactly what's interfering with your scheduled time to write and determine whether you can adjust it. If not, schedule a new writing time. You may even want to set different times for different days of the week to accommodate family or work.

You probably need to be persistent if…

- you're not getting your writing done because you're allowing other things to distract you, and
- you're feeling guilty or badly about it.

Persistence is what you need to overcome ingrained habits and establish new ones. Stick with the routine you set up, and renew your efforts to overcome your vulnerability to distractions or any other similar issues you may be experiencing.

Most of the time, you can use your feelings to determine which approach will work best. When life events get in the way, it's normal to feel up against a wall trying to manage everything, and this is when you need flexibility. Maybe you need to break up your scheduled hour of writing into four fifteen-minute stretches that fit between events, or you might consider keeping a notebook or typing app handy so you can write whenever an open moment appears. You could also use your phone to record your story and then transcribe the recordings to text when you have time. You may have to settle for a less-than-optimal setup for a while, but it's better than abandoning your writing altogether.

Being flexible is particularly helpful during difficult life events such as a loss of a job, death in the family, or serious health issue. It's easy to think you should drop your writing when things get rough, but your writing is most important at these times. Remember that you are a creative person, and creating is part of what makes you feel whole. Writing will help you relieve stress and regain your sense of self when your world starts to fall apart. Finding a way to fit it in during trying times may well be one of your most important coping techniques.

When you feel guilty or like you're letting yourself down, however, it's time to employ persistence. For instance, if you set aside Sundays, Tuesdays, and Thursdays after lunch to write for an hour, and you haven't done it and you feel guilty, it's probably because you allowed something else to distract you. Whatever it was probably "seemed" worthwhile at the time, but in hindsight, you realized you would have rather spent the time writing.

There's a subtle difference between events that require you to be flexible or persistent, but the more you practice, the more you'll be able to tell when you need to apply one skill or the other. Here's a chart to help you out.

| **Persistence—try again!** | **Flexibility—try something new.** |
|---|---|
| I missed my writing time last week because my boss called me in for an unscheduled meeting. (Try again the next week—this might have been a one-time thing.) | I missed my writing time three days in a row because my mom ended up in the hospital. (Revamp your schedule so you can care for your mom.) |
| During my writing times, I get easily distracted by social media. (Shut the apps down when it's time to write.) | Every time I try to write I nearly fall asleep because I'm tired. (Reschedule your writing slot to high-energy times of the day.) |
| Once my writing time starts, it takes me a long time to focus on my story. I stare at the blank page for ten minutes or more. (Re-read Chapter 7 and keep at it.) | My wife got a new job and now needs me to care for the baby at night. (Find a new time when you can write now that your schedule has changed.) |
| I keep pushing the snooze button and don't get up when it's time to write. (Put the alarm clock across the room so you have to get up to turn it off.) | I'm working on a different kind of story than I've done before and my creativity seems dead during my current writing time. (Try other times of the day when you may be feeling more creative, or try writing in another location.) |

| My family keeps interrupting me when I'm writing. (Shut the door and put a "do not disturb" sign on it.) | I got a new job and now I have to commute for forty-five minutes one way every day. (Try something new like talking out your stories on the road, or writing at work before or after hours.) |

## The Emotional Component

If you're still not sure whether to choose flexibility or persistence, let your emotions be your guide. Look back over the last week and rate your writing time—were you productive or not? If you weren't, ask yourself how that made you feel. What emotional response bubbles up when you review your week?

The following feelings are likely to indicate that you didn't live up to your commitments, and you need to be more persistent:

- guilt
- shame
- disappointment
- personal frustration

The following feelings are likely to indicate that other things in life are interfering with your creative time, and you need to be flexible:

- exhaustion
- fear

- overwhelm
- confusion
- grief

Once you can more clearly understand what your emotions are telling you, you'll have a better chance of applying the right solution.

Just don't expect that once you have a routine that works it's going to work forever. Life is full of change, and you must change with it. Re-evaluate your schedule and your routines regularly and make adjustments when needed, and you'll always have the upper hand on maintaining productive writing times.

CHAPTER 21

# FIND WRITER SOLUTIONS

"Physician, heal thyself," the proverb says, and so we must.

Only in this case, it's, "Writer, figure out thine own issues." Many times, when you're struggling with a story or other writing project, you need to find a craft solution. By that I mean you need to learn more about setting, dialogue, and plot; hire editors to help you spot your weaknesses; and attend educational workshops to help you break through any difficulties and start making progress again.

But sometimes, you may become blocked on a project or find yourself unable to progress at all because of an issue that has nothing to do with craft. It's at these times that you must find writer solutions.

A few months ago, for example, my writing stalled. I was working on my next novel and I was stuck. In the middle of the second draft, I had a quiet voice telling me that something wasn't working, but I didn't know what. I turned to craft books and studied plot and theme. I jotted down notes. I spent time in the shower and the car thinking over every part of the story. Then I went back and tried again.

After a series of starts and stops, I was thoroughly frustrated.

Things *still* weren't working. The story just wasn't flowing and I didn't know why.

Writers come up against these kinds of issues all the time. Our progress stalls, and we can't find the answers we need in the craft of writing. Meanwhile, our productivity tanks. Unfortunately, while you can hire a book doctor to help cure what ails your story, there is no such physician to cure your writer-self. The responsibility for getting back on your feet (or your fingers) and restoring your progress lies squarely with the person in the mirror.

## Discover What's Really Blocking You

We all have habitual behaviors we've developed without really being aware of them. Finding out why you're doing something or feeling something is key to making successful changes. That applies to any area of life, but particularly to writing, finding time to write, and maximizing productivity. If you set up a new writing schedule, for example, and then get no writing done, or if you're stuck on your story and you don't know why, you have to stop and do some detective work. You have to find out what's going on.

Unfortunately, that's often easier said than done.

Let me return to my issue of being stuck on my novel. I thought I knew what the problem was—I was struggling with plot. So I went back to the drawing board and studied plot. Then I returned to the story, and within a few days of writing, got stuck again. All that research on craft didn't help. Not one bit.

As writers, we so often think the solution lies in craft. It makes sense. If a carpenter creates a desk that wobbles, obviously he's going to go back to the drafting table and find out where he made a miscalculation. Writers think they can do the same thing—go back and find the issue in the story itself.

Sometimes this works, but sometimes—I'd even venture to say more often than not—the problem isn't a craft problem, it's in the writer's head and heart. He is facing a writer problem, and only by solving it can he successfully solve the story problem.

## Try Something Different

So there I was. I did all that research and studying and experimenting and trying, and was still stuck on my novel. Fortunately, I just happened to have my yearly vacation coming up, so I decided to take a break for about twelve days. (Remember my suggestion in Chapter 11 about taking breaks—here's an example of how helpful that can be.) I walked the beach, hiked through forests, enjoyed some horseback riding, did some seaside shopping, and ate several delicious meals. Slowly, I started to more clearly hear the whisperings of my creative muse.

Here's what she told me to write this book.

I got the strong feeling it was time to put my thoughts about time management, productivity, and creative priorities into book form. The idea had been percolating in my mind for years, but suddenly it was knocking loudly against my psyche, saying *now now now*. I balked at the idea, because I knew if I followed the muse's instructions and worked on this book, I would have to put my novel aside for a while. I worried that if I stepped away from it, I would lose the story altogether, and it would end up abandoned in the backlogs of my computer.

By the time the vacation was over, though, my path was clear. When I got back home, I started working on this book first thing every morning. I tried to get in some time on my novel at night, but most of the time that didn't work because I was just too tired to muster the energy to face this difficult novel that was kicking my butt.

This book, meanwhile, took off like wildfire. The more I worked on it, the more I wanted to work on it. I started feeling the writing spark again, and my creative muse sat up and smiled. I was having fun, instead of bashing my head against the wall. It felt great! Once again, I was enjoying a sense of accomplishment, and felt I was following the right path.

Here's where the surprise comes in, and here's the point I'm trying to make: Within about a month of making this change, the light bulb went off where my novel is concerned. I hadn't made any real progress on it for several months, but one night it dawned on me that I might tell my novel in a completely different way. Within a few days, I was moving forward again with my new approach, even while continuing progress on this book. I solved my problem of being stuck, *not* with a craft solution, but with a *writer* solution. By following my own creative inclinations, I freed my muse to do what she does best.

## Symptoms of a Writer Problem

Writing problems of all sorts are frustrating. It's natural to want to find the easy way out. Sometimes books or posts or courses or mentors can help you, but you're a creative person, which means that sometimes the only answers are those inside of you.

I'm not saying there aren't craft solutions to any problems you may be facing. If your study doesn't open the door for you, though, it's time to define the problem in terms of your writer-self, and to thereby find a writer solution.

Symptoms of a writer problem include:

1. Writer's block
2. Lack of excitement about writing, or avoiding writing time
3. Difficulty finding time to write
4. A story lacking excitement or suspense
5. Failure to progress on a story for months at a time
6. Stagnant writing skills—you aren't getting any better
7. Constant excuses for not getting your writing done
8. Difficulty figuring out what to write about
9. Feeling like writing is boring
10. Apathy—assuming no one will care about what you write, anyway

These and other similar issues are often writer problems, not craft problems. Though number four could potentially be a craft problem, it is often the product of a writer who has yet to tap into her inner passion and transcribe it onto the page. It can also be a symptom of a writer who has gotten tired of writing in one particular genre, or who is just burned out.

The challenge comes in figuring out what your writing problem is. That, after all, is key to being able to find a solution. I was suffering from problem number five in the list above—failing to make progress on my story. It took me months to finally realize what my muse was trying to tell me, and to get out of my own way and let my creativity flow. It's easy to get bogged down in the details, especially when life is racing by so quickly and there's so much noise around you all the time.

I've got some possible solutions for you. The bottom line is that you probably don't know yourself as well as you think. Sometimes you have to take a step back and gain some distance to find out what's really going on. That takes time, commitment, and a willingness to make some inquiries into your writer-self.

### Time Treasure

## 5 Ways to Identify Your Writer Problem

I'm focusing on the problem, here, because once you can spell it out, you'll find the solution easily presents itself. That's what happened when I realized it was time to write this book. When I started letting it out of my head and getting it down on the computer, my creative brain opened up, leaving room for the solution to my novel to appear.

You, too, will be able to easily find the writer solution when you can clearly identify the problem.

**1. Get away from it all.**
This remains the best solution to most writer problems. You have to get away and get quiet to truly hear what the muse is trying to tell you. She speaks very softly, and most of the time you just can't hear her.

You don't necessarily need to take a vacation by the beach to make this happen (although I highly recommend it!). A weekend away in a new location could work. Writer's conferences and retreats may also do the trick. Getting away from your normal location and out of your normal routine remains the most effective solution.

**2. Ask the muse what it wants.**
Just ask the muse what's going on. Start with a blank piece of paper or a new Word document and write across the top:

"What does my creative heart desire right now?"

Then spend about ten to fifteen minutes free writing to answer that question. No matter what, write until the time is up. Then review what you've written and see if it sparks something inside you. You may discover that your real creative desires are different from what you thought they were.

Let's say you scheduled your lunch hour for writing a few weeks ago, but even though you've gone to the cafeteria and sat there with your keyboard for thirty minutes every day, you've got little to show for it. The time isn't working, and you don't know why. You free write on the question above and find that your creative heart wants you *out* of that job.

That realization may frighten you. The idea of quitting can be scary for anyone, and is probably why you haven't admitted it to yourself until now. What your heart really wants is to quit a boring job that offers few rewards. Yet you need the paycheck.

The good news is that this exercise clarifies the problem. Maybe deep in your mind, you thought that writing while on a job you hate left you no hope of ever leaving that job. Maybe somehow your unconscious mind connected the two—the job you hate, and your writing time—thereby blocking your creative process.

This opens your eyes, and allows you to envision some solutions. Maybe you need to separate writing time from work, explore other ways to cut back on your hours, or plan for your eventual exit from the place. Perhaps all you need is to give yourself some hope that you won't have to spend forever in this unfulfilling job.

The point is to allow yourself to *feel what you feel*. Just because you'd like to quit your job doesn't mean you have to. Acknowledging your real feelings about any issue gives you the opportunity to consider solutions, and meanwhile releases an emotional blockage. That may be all you need to open the lines of communication with your writing muse so you can start producing again.

If there's anything in your free writing that renews your excitement about writing, pursue it however you can.

### 3. Find out what you're feeling.

Writer problems are often emotional problems. Therefore, it's important to find out what emotions you may be burying when you're troubleshooting an issue. Keeping a journal helps. Read through the following list of questions. When one triggers a reaction in you, spend a few minutes answering it in your journal to see if you can hone in on what is blocking your creative flow.

- Is fear or self-doubt rattling in your ear? Are you afraid your writing won't be "good enough?"

- Are you speaking up for yourself and putting your priorities first, or are you caving in to others' desires?

- Is there a naysayer in your world, trying to tell you that you can't do it? Might this naysayer be someone from your past?

- Are you feeling guilty about taking time to write? If so, why?

- Are you still allowing work to come first, resulting in no energy to write?

- What's causing your frustration? Is it in your power to change it?

- Are you writing what you really *want* to write?

- What words would you use to describe how you're feeling about this issue?

- Is your writing bringing you joy? If not, why not?

- Is there something going on that you're afraid to face?

- Do you suffer from any physical ailments (fatigue, illness, headaches, etc.) that are getting in the way of writing?

- Do you think too much of outside rewards (publication,

royalties, etc.)? Are your expectations so high they're stifling your work?

Once you've answered the question you chose, review your answer. See if it sparks any ideas for solutions. If not, come back to this list again in a few days, and answer a different question. Continue the process until you experience a breakthrough.

### 4. Focus only on your behaviors.

We are all guilty of watching others and then judging them by their actions. With ourselves, though, we tend to focus less on actions and more on feelings and intentions. I may hold good thoughts about my neighbors, for example, but rarely speak to them or interact with them. In my mind, I'm a good neighbor, but perhaps in their minds, I come off as aloof and uncaring.

They judge me by what I do. I judge myself by my thoughts and intentions. This is how we fool ourselves. Most of us create self-portraits that fail to reflect who we really are. Only by examining our *actions* can we get a more accurate picture.

Take a moment, then, and examine *only your behavior* when it comes to writing. Ask yourself what you are actually *doing*. Maybe you intend to write, but you've yet to get any words down on paper. So in truth, you're *not writing*, and that's a writer problem.

Maybe you're excited about your story idea in your mind, but you actually haven't gotten any farther than the first page in several weeks. In your head you have a complete story, but you have written only one page. So the truth is, you've barely started. Ask yourself why you haven't made more progress. Maybe this idea really doesn't excite you as much as you thought. Maybe you told your publisher you'd be happy to complete another romance book, but then as the deadline looms, you realize you've gotten little done on it. In your mind, there have been too many distractions—health problems in the family, a remodel on the kitchen, etc. You intended to get it done, but you've been swamped with other things.

Regardless of what you tell yourself, your behavior exposes the truth: you are avoiding writing this book. That's the problem you must address.

By isolating and examining only your behaviors, you can discover the reason behind the writer problems you may be facing. Then you can find a solution.

## 5. Be honest.

It's often difficult to be honest about why we're not getting our writing done, because the answer usually reveals something we don't like to admit about ourselves, or something we're scared to face.

Maybe you've gotten yourself into a story that just isn't going to work. You've rewritten it again and again and it still isn't fitting together like you know it should. You could get honest and face the fact that it may be time to put it away and try something else, but that's difficult because you've

> worked on it for so long. But it may be the only way you can move forward.
>
> Maybe you *really* want to write but your partner is unsupportive. You don't want to admit this to yourself, so you write in secret, or you pursue your passion on your own without sharing it with the person you love. Over time, the situation wears on you, and you start to resent your partner's attitude, all the while wishing you could do more.
>
> Maybe you're simply trying to do too much. You thought you could manage your job, family responsibilities, volunteering, and writing, but the truth is that something has to give.
>
> Being honest with yourself requires courage, but it's usually the only way you can get around certain issues. If you're not

getting your writing done, instead of always blaming your busy schedule ("I just don't have time!"), ask yourself if there is something you're denying about your situation, and take a good, hard look at the honest truth. Once you've accurately identified the problem, you can find real solutions that will get you back on the path to enjoying a creative life.

## Take Your Writer Self Seriously

One more thought on finding writer solutions—give yourself time. These things often take weeks if not months or longer to work themselves out. Use that time to reflect, free write, journal, meditate, and get away if you can.

The point is that you need to take your writer self just as seriously as you take the writing craft. You are a complex individual. Scientists have been studying creativity for years and have only just scratched the surface. Mood, environment, personal history, physical wellness, mental wellness, education, self-esteem, and much more all come into the picture when you're making something from scratch, be it a novel, painting, sculpture, or musical composition.

Finding time to write—and tapping into the creative muse while doing so—is about so much more than just finding thirty minutes of free time. Everything is involved. Everything I've talked about so far in this book, and everything else that may be going on in your life right now, can affect your productivity and accomplishment.

Allow yourself to look at the whole picture when troubleshooting difficulties. Consider your whole writer self and you'll be far more likely to find a solution that will really work.

CHAPTER 22

# GET GRIT

When I was young, *True Grit* starring John Wayne and Kim Darby was one of my favorite movies. I admired Darby's character, Mattie Ross, and how brave she was in her quest to bring her father's killer to justice. The scene that really stayed with me, though, involved Mattie's horse, Little Blackie.

After Mattie is bitten by a rattlesnake, John Wayne's character, Rooster Cogburn, has no choice but to try to get her to the hospital in time to save her life. The problem is it's a long ride, and it's all up to Little Blackie. I watched that horse run carrying both Rooster and Mattie over miles and miles of vast western prairie, Rooster urging him on, until the white foam welled up on his chest and the saliva dripped from his mouth, and still he ran until finally he dropped to the ground, exhausted, and never got up again.

As a horse lover, that scene was very traumatic for me. I saw Little Blackie as the character that personified true grit, and grieved with Mattie when she found out he was dead. As an adult, I understand that Mattie was the survivor in the story, as she made it through treatment and went on to live a successful life, but when I think of grit, I still see that animal running and running and running with his owner near death on his back.

If there's one thing we all love in our story characters, it's grit. You probably had some childhood heroes of your own that you admired for this very reason. You cheered when they overcame their difficulties and succeeded in their goals. You were inspired when they rallied and clawed their way to the finish line. You imagined yourself in their shoes, and wondered if you could do the same.

Now, it's time to become your own hero.

Courage and resolve. Strength of character. Firmness of mind and spirit. Unyielding courage in the face of hardship or danger. These are all definitions of the word "grit." What you have to find out is if you have it, and if not, how you can develop it, because it's one characteristic you need as a writer. When the chips are down, it may be the only one you can count on to help you succeed.

## How Gritty Are You?

Rate yourself on the following statements from 1 to 5, with 1 being "very much like me," and 5 being "not like me at all."

- I have overcome setbacks to conquer an important challenge.
- Setbacks don't discourage me.
- I have achieved a goal that took years of work.

These questions come from a grit questionnaire developed by Angela Duckworth, Ph.D., professor of psychology at the University of Pennsylvania. After teaching math in middle school and high school for a while, she wondered why some students accomplished more than others even if they were equal in intelligence.

Together with her colleagues, she developed this questionnaire and then had several students complete it. She found out that so-called "gritty" individuals attained higher levels of education, had higher GPAs, and were more likely to complete summer training at a military academy than less gritty individuals. Overall, grit seemed to have more influence on success than even IQ levels.

This isn't just about hard work, but about focused, long-term effort toward a goal. Imagine two children, for example, each with equal musical talent who practice with the same focused intensity. In the end, what will separate one from the other is the duration of effort—accumulated hours devoted to musical study. Duckworth and colleagues found that the child who continues to practice the piano will eventually surpass the equally gifted child who divides her time between the piano and the saxophone.

This is the ultimate reason why finding time to write is *so critical to your success as a writer.* The more time you can devote true focused effort and concentration to your craft the more likely you are to reach your goals.

**Grit Trumps Talent**

Writing is a long-haul business that takes years to yield results, and along the way there are a lot of ups and downs. If you have grit, though, you will succeed where others won't. You will continue to practice even when it gets tough. You'll find time to write no matter what, and you'll seek out ways to improve. You'll stay committed to your goal year after year.

When you think about it, this is great news. You may wonder if you have enough creative talent to "make it," but studies on grit suggest you don't need to worry about it. In the end, it's not the most important thing. If you have the desire to write, and you're willing to put in the time and effort it takes, your ability to endure will increase your odds of eventually succeeding more than talent will, because grit trumps talent.

Duckworth and colleague Lauren Eskreis-Winkler wrote in the *Observer* in 2013: "Our research suggests that prodigious talent is no guarantee of grit. In fact, in most samples, grit and talent are either orthogonal or slightly negatively correlated."

Remember—in their studies, it wasn't the talented people that were the most successful. It was the gritty ones.

## Developing Grit

If you're not sure you're as gritty as you'd like to be, you may wonder if you can develop this skill. Scientists say you can, and here are some of the best ways to do it:

1. **Find time to write.** The more you write, the better you'll get at it, and research shows that we're more likely to stick with things we're good at.

2. **Find meaning in your writing.** The more you can connect with "why" you write, the closer your relationship will be to your writing. This is why it pays to choose the project that matters most to you, over the one you feel is more marketable.

3. **Seek out ways to improve.** Attend workshops. Take online courses. Hire an editor. The writing process must include getting feedback and learning to overcome your weaknesses. This sort of work feeds the hope that you will get better as you go, and that hope is the motivation you need to hang in there. Even if you're an experienced writer, if you want to develop grit, keep challenging yourself and reaching higher.

4. **Spend time with other gritty people.** These people don't have to be writers. All that matters is that they've overcome hardships to reach their goals. Let them inspire you.

5. **Face your fears.** Fear is something we all wrestle with throughout life. Make it a regular habit to reflect on what scares you, and seek out ways to overcome those fears. As you do this again and again, you'll develop the grit you need to overcome things that may scare you in the future.

True grit requires a lot of desire, motivation, and hard work, but if you want to be a writer for life, it's absolutely required. No matter where you start out on the grit scale, you can develop this characteristic as you go, which will allow you to make even bigger leaps forward in the future.

CHAPTER 23

# ANSWER YOUR CALLING

I READ A STUDY once in which the researchers concluded that having a calling (such as writing or another creative endeavor) and not following it was worse than having no calling at all.

Psychologists from the University of South Florida surveyed nearly 400 American academic professionals, asking them questions about their careers and how they felt about them. They wondered whether the professionals found purpose and meaning in their jobs, or if there were other careers they were drawn to but had never pursued.

You could ask yourself the same thing right now: Does your job fill your life with purpose and meaning, or are you drawn to another calling? Are you pursuing that calling, or has it gone unanswered?

Most of the study results were not surprising. Those participants who felt they were fulfilling their dreams as professors scored higher on job satisfaction, personal well-being, and health. Those who didn't feel they were going after any particular "calling" didn't score quite as high. What was surprising, though, was that the participants who had the worst scores on all three of these life measures were those who felt like they *still had an unanswered calling*.

In other words, those people who didn't really think about having a "dream job" or occupation were actually better off than those who *did* feel like their dream job was out there, but they hadn't gone after it yet.

If you feel called to write and you're not doing it, you're literally putting your health and well-being at risk. You're getting less out of life than you could be. I would even say that as a person, you *are* less than you could be, because you're not fulfilling your potential.

I'm a firm believer in the idea that we are called to certain activities for a reason. It usually has to do with who we are as human beings, and who we will become in the future. You don't know if your work will be seen and celebrated, if you'll be a bestseller or Pulitzer Prize winner, or if you'll get a publisher for your next project, but you do know that if you leave this calling unanswered, or even if you pursue it only halfway, you will feel incomplete. If, on the other hand, you give it all you've got day after day, no matter what happens with your work in the outside world, you will feel a renewed sense of peace and calm, because your soul's calling is being heard.

Leaving a calling unanswered is like ignoring a rock in your shoe. You're feeling that rock now. Embrace that feeling. Let it hurt. Let it remind you that *this is important*. Whatever else is going on in your life, you've been called to write, and for your own personal development and happiness, you must answer that calling not just today, but every day as long as it whispers in your ear.

Answer it before doing the dishes and after putting the kids to bed. Answer it first thing in the morning, or last thing at night. Answer it during your lunch hour, on the train ride home, or on a quiet weekend afternoon. Answer it, a little bit every day, until you have a regular, reliable conversation going on.

Answer that calling to write, and allow it to expand your life and your world in all the hundreds of magical ways that writing does. Good luck!

## NOTE FROM THE AUTHOR

Reviews are gold to authors! If you've enjoyed this book, would you consider rating it and reviewing it on www.Amazon.com and/or www.Goodreads.com?

If you'd like to keep your productivity going and learn more about empowering your health, wellness, and creativity, sign up for the free Writing and Wellness newsletter. You'll get access to inspirational and motivational posts, additional training, future ebooks, and more. Sign up here: www.writingandwellness.com/newsletter/

# REFERENCES

## CHAPTER 1

Abrams, Dennis. "How Much Do Writers Earn? Less Than You Think." Publishing Perspectives. Last modified January 20, 2014. http://publishingperspectives.com/2014/01/how-much-do-writers-earn-less-than-you-think/#.V_5yWVszwy4.

Weinberg, Dana B., and Jeremy Greenfield. What Advantages Do Traditional Publishers Offer Authors | Digital Book World Store. Digital Book World, n.d. http://store.digitalbookworld.com/advantages-traditional-publishers-offer-authors-t3591.

## CHAPTER 2

Brown, Scott W. "Time perception and attention: The effects of prospective versus retrospective paradigms and task demands on perceived duration." *Perception & Psychophysics* 38, no. 2 (1985), 115-124. doi:10.3758/bf03198848.

Droit-Volet, Sylvie, Sophie L. Fayolle, and Sandrine Gil. "Emotion and Time Perception: Effects of Film-Induced Mood." *Frontiers in Integrative Neuroscience* 5 (2011). doi:10.3389/fnint.2011.00033.

McLoughlin, Dr. Aoife. "Wired Society Speeds Up Brains ... and Time - JCU Australia." Home - JCU Australia. Last modified November 19, 2015. https://www.jcu.edu.au/news/releases/wired-society-speeds-up-brains-and-time.

Sucala, Madalina, Bari Scheckner, and Daniel David. "Psychological Time: Interval Length Judgments and Subjective Passage of Time Judgments." *Current Psychology Letters* 26, no. 2 (2010). http://cpl.revues.org/4998.

## CHAPTER 3

Lightman, Alan. "Alan Lightman On Boycotting E-Mail: Excerpted from an interview with Matthew Herper on Oct. 7, 2005." *Forbes*, October 24, 2005. http://www.forbes.com/2005/10/19/lightman-technology-email-comm05-cx_mh_1024lightman.html.

Elpidorou, Andreas. "The bright side of boredom." *Frontiers in Psychology* 5 (2014). doi:10.3389/fpsyg.2014.01245.

Gasper, Karen, and Brianna L. Middlewood. "Approaching novel thoughts: Understanding why elation and boredom promote associative thought more than distress and relaxation." *Journal of Experimental Social Psychology* 52 (2014), 50-57. doi:10.1016/j.jesp.2013.12.007.

Goodrich, Terry. "Baylor University || Media Communications || News." Media Communications | Baylor University. Last modified August 27, 2014. https://www.baylor.edu/mediacommunications/news.php?action=story&story=145864.

Gorlick, Adam. "Media Multitaskers Pay Mental Price, Stanford Study Shows." Stanford News. Last modified August 24, 2009. http://news.stanford.edu/2009/08/24/multitask-research-study-082409/.

Gregg, Melissa. "The Productivity Obsession." *The Atlantic*, November 13, 2015. http://www.theatlantic.com/business/archive/2015/11/be-more-productive/415821/.

Hampton, Keith, Lee Rainie, Weixu Lu, Inyoung Shin, and Kristen Purcell. "Psychological Stress and Social Media Use | Pew Research Center." Pew Research Center: Internet, Science & Tech. Last modified January 15, 2015. http://www.pewinternet.org/2015/01/15/psychological-stress-and-social-media-use-2/.

Levitin, Daniel J. "Why the modern world is bad for your brain." *The Guardian*, January 18, 2015. https://www.theguardian.com/science/2015/jan/18/modern-world-bad-for-brain-daniel-j-levitin-organized-mind-information-overload.

Loder, Vanessa. "Why Multi-Tasking Is Worse Than Marijuana For Your IQ." *Forbes*, June 11, 2004. http://www.forbes.com/sites/vanessaloder/2014/06/11/why-multi-tasking-is-worse-than-marijuana-for-your-iq/#30c548444e51.

Mann, Sandi, and Rebekah Cadman. "Does Being Bored Make Us More Creative?" *Creativity Research Journal* 26, no. 2 (2014), 165-173. doi:10.1080/10400419.2014.901073.

"Multitasking: Switching costs." American Psychological Association. Last modified March 20, 2006. http://www.apa.org/research/action/multitask.aspx.

Tartakovsky, Margarita. "Overcoming Information Overload." World of Psychology. Last modified January 21, 2013. http://psychcentral.com/blog/archives/2013/01/21/overcoming-information-overload/.

Wall, Matthew. "Smartphone Stress: Are You a Victim of 'Always On' Culture?" *BBC News*, August 14, 2014. http://www.bbc.com/news/business-28686235.

## CHAPTER 4

Besedeš Tibor, Cary Deck, Sudipta Sarangi, and Mikhael Shor. "Reducing Choice Overload without Reducing Choices." *Review of Economics and Statistics* 97, no. 4 (2015), 793-802. doi:10.1162/rest_a_00506.

Iyengar, Sheena S., and Mark R. Lepper. "When choice is demotivating: Can one desire too much of a good thing?" *Journal of Personality and Social Psychology* 79, no. 6 (2000), 995-1006. doi:10.1037//0022-3514 79.6.995.

Toon, John. "Choosing a Cell Phone, Prescription Drug Plan or New Car? Read This First." Georgia Tech News. Last modified February 3, 2015. http://www.news.gatech.edu/2015/02/03/choosing-cell-phone-prescription-drug-plan-or-new-car-read-first.

Vohs, Kathleen D., Roy F. Baumeister, Brandon J. Schmeichel, Jean M. Twenge, Noelle M. Nelson, and Dianne M. Tice. "Making choices impairs subsequent self-control: A limited-resource account of decision making, self-regulation, and active initiative." *Journal of Personality and Social Psychology* 94, no. 5 (2008), 883-898. doi:10.1037/0022-3514.94.5.383.

Poldrack, Russell A. "What is Loss Aversion?" *Scientific American Mind*, n.d. https://www.scientificamerican.com/article/what-is-loss-aversion/.

Tversky, A., and D. Kahneman. "The framing of decisions and the psychology of choice." *Science* 211, no. 4481 (1981), 453-458. doi:10.1126/science.7455683.

## CHAPTER 5

Goudzwaard, B., and Josina Van Nuis Zylstra. *Capitalism and Progress: A Diagnosis of Western Society*. Toronto, Canada: Wedge Pub. Foundation, 1979.

Lam, Bourree. "The Wasted Workday." *The Atlantic*, December 4, 2014. http://www.theatlantic.com/business/archive/2014/12/the-wasted-workday/383380.

Mark, Gloria, Shamsi T. Iqbal, Mary Czerwinski, and Paul Johns. "Bored Mondays and focused afternoons." *Proceedings of the 32nd annual ACM conference on Human factors in computing systems - CHI '14*, April 2014, 3025-3034. doi:10.1145/2556288.2557204.

Silverman, Rachel Emma. "The Hidden Pleasures of Busywork." *The Wall Street Journal*, March 3, 2014. http://blogs.wsj.com/atwork/2014/03/03/the-hidden-pleasures-of-busywork/.

Vedantam, Shankar. "How Scarcity Trap Affects Our Thinking, Behavior." *NPR*, January 2, 2014. http://www.npr.org/2014/01/02/259082836/how-scarcity-mentaly-affects-our-thinking-behavior.

Zeigarnik, Bluma. "On finished and unfinished tasks." In *A Source Book of Gestalt Psychology*, edited by Willis Davis Ellis, 300-314. London: Paul, Trench, Trubner, 1938. http://psycnet.apa.org/psycinfo/2007-10344-025.

Zeigarnik, Bluma. "On Finished and Unfinished Tasks." *Psychologische Forschung*, 1927. http://codeblab.com/wp-content/uploads/2009/12/On-Finished-and-Unfinished-Tasks.pdf.

## CHAPTER 6

Bureau of Labor Statistics. "American time use survey." U.S. Bureau of Labor Statistics. Last modified 2012. https://www.bls.gov/tus/tables/a1_2013.pdf.

Chang, Lulu. "Americans Spend An Alarming 4.7 Hours On Their Phones." Digital Trends. Last modified June 13, 2015. http://www.digitaltrends.com/mobile/informate-report-social-media-smartphone-use/.

Chui, Michael, James Manyika, Jacques Bughin, Richard Dobbs, Charles Roxburgh, Hugo Sarrazin, Geoffrey Sands, and Magdalena Westergren. *The Social Economy: Unlocking Value and Productivity Through Social Technologies | McKinsey & Company*. McKinsey Global Institute, 2012. http://www.mckinsey.com/industries/high-tech/our-insights/the-social-economy.

Coker, Brent L. "Freedom to surf: the positive effects of workplace Internet leisure browsing." *New Technology, Work and Employment* 26, no. 3 (November 2011), 238-247. doi:10.1111/j.1468-005x.2011.00272.x.

Foroughi, C. K., N. E. Werner, E. T. Nelson, and D. A. Boehm-Davis. "Do Interruptions Affect Quality of Work?" *Human Factors: The Journal of the Human Factors and Ergonomics Society* 56, no. 7 (August 2014), 1262-1271. doi:10.1177/0018720814531786.

Hinckley, David. "Average American watches 5 hours of TV per day, report shows." *NY Daily News* (New York). March 5, 2014. http://www.nydailynews.com/life-style/average-american-watches-5-hours-tv-day-article-1.1711954.

Keadle, Sarah K., Steven C. Moore, Joshua N. Sampson, Qian Xiao, Demetrius Albanes, and Charles E. Matthews. "Causes of Death Associated With Prolonged TV Viewing." *American Journal of Preventive Medicine* 49, no. 6 (December 2015), 811–821. doi.org/10.1016/j.amepre.2015.05.023.

Killgore, William D. "Effects of sleep deprivation on cognition." *Progress in Brain Research*, no. 185 (2010), 105-129. doi:10.1016/b978-0-444-53702-7.00007-5.

*A Look at Commuting Patterns in the United States from the American Community Survey*. U.S. Census Bureau, 2013. https://www.census.gov/content/dam/Census/newsroom/c-span/2013/20130308_cspan_commuting.pdf.

Mander, Jason. "Daily Time Spent on Social Networks Rises to 1.72 Hours." GlobalWebIndex | Know Your Audience™. Last modified January 26, 2015. https://www.globalwebindex.net/blog/daily-time-spent-on-social-networks-rises-to-1-72-hours.

Pattison, Kermit. "Worker, Interrupted: The Cost of Task Switching | Business + Innovation." *Fast Company*. Last modified July 28, 2008. https://www.fastcompany.com/944128/worker-interrupted-cost-task-switching.

Radicati, Sara. *Email Statistics Report, 2011-2015*. Palo Alto, California: The Radicati Group, n.d. http://www.radicati.com/wp/wp-content/uploads/2011/05/Email-Statistics-Report-2011-2015-Executive-Summary.pdf.

Stewart, James B. "Facebook Has 50 Minutes of Your Time Each Day. It Wants More." *New York Times* (New York), May 5, 2016. http://www.nytimes.

com/2016/05/06/business/facebook-bends-the-rules-of-audience-engagement-to-its-advantage.html?_r=0.

## CHAPTER 7

Braverman, Eric. "You're Getting Dumber as You Age: Here's How to Slow the Decline." *The Atlantic*, February 3, 2012. http://www.theatlantic.com/health/archive/2012/02/youre-getting-dumber-as-you-age-heres-how-to-slow-the-decline/252061/.

Dolegui, Arielle S. "The Impact of Listening to Music on Cognitive Performance." *Inquiries Journal* 5, no. 9 (2013), 1-2. http://www.inquiriesjournal.com/articles/762/the-impact-of-listening-to-music-on-cognitive-performance.

Nöteberg, Staffan, and Francesco Cirillo. *Pomodoro Technique Illustrated: The Easy Way to Do More in Less Time*. Raleigh, N.C.: Pragmatic Bookshelf, 2009.

Riddle, David R. "Chapter 1: Changes in Cognitive Function in Human Aging." In *Brain Aging: Models, Methods, and Mechanisms*. Boca Raton: CRC Press, 2007.

Rock, David. "Easily Distracted: Why It's Hard to Focus, and What to Do About It." *Psychology Today*, October 4, 2009. https://www.psychologytoday.com/blog/your-brain-work/200910/easily-distracted-why-its-hard-focus-and-what-do-about-it.

Rosen, Ph.D., Larry. "Attention Alert: A Study on Distraction Reveals Some Surprises." Dr. Larry Rosen - Research Psychologist and Educator. Last modified April 9, 2012. https://www.psychologytoday.com/blog/rewired-the-psychology-technology/201204/attention-alert-study-distraction-reveals-some.

Thompson, Joseph J., Mark R. Blair, and Andrew J. Henrey. "Over the Hill at 24: Persistent Age-Related Cognitive-Motor Decline in Reaction Times in an Ecologically Valid Video Game Task Begins in Early Adulthood." *PLoS ONE* 9, no. 4 (April 2014), e94215. doi:10.1371/journal.pone.0094215.

University of Connecticut. "Cranky Today? Even Mild Dehydration Can Alter Our Moods Science News." EurekAlert!. Last modified February 17, 2012. http://www.eurekalert.org/pub_releases/2012-02/uoc-cte021712.php.

Watson, Leon. "Humans Have Shorter Attention Span Than

Goldfish, Thanks to Smartphones." *The Telegraph* (London), May 15, 2015. http://www.telegraph.co.uk/science/2016/03/12/humans-have-shorter-attention-span-than-goldfish-thanks-to-smart/.

## CHAPTER 8

Collingwood, Jane. "What's Your Time Perspective?" Psych Central. Accessed June 17, 2017. https://psychcentral.com/lib/whats-your-time-perspective/.

Lam, Bourree. "Clocks Make Workers Less Creative." *The Atlantic*, October 6, 2014. https://www.theatlantic.com/business/archive/2014/10/clocks-make-workers-less-creative/381064/.

MacDonald, Fiona. "Science Says That Technology is Speeding Up Our Brains' Perception of Time." ScienceAlert. Last modified November 19, 2015. http://www.sciencealert.com/research-suggests-that-technology-is-speeding-up-our-perception-of-time.

Newport, Frank. "Americans' Perceived Time Crunch No Worse Than in Past | Gallup." Gallup.com. Last modified December/January 31, 2015. http://www.gallup.com/poll/187982/americans-perceived-time-crunch-no-worse-past.aspx.

Sellier, Anne-Laure, and Tamar Avnet. "So what if the clock strikes? Scheduling style, control, and well-being." *Journal of Personality and Social Psychology* 107, no. 5 (2014): 791-808. doi:10.1037/a0038051.

Zimbardo P. and Boyd J. Putting Time in Perspective: A Valid, Reliable Individual-Difference Metric. *The Journal of Personality and Social Psychology*, Vol. 77, 1999, pp. 1271-88.

## CHAPTER 9

Ferriss, Tim. "Why (and How) Creative People Need to Say 'No' | The Blog of Author Tim Ferriss." Tim Ferriss and The 4-Hour Workweek. Last modified July 31, 2013. http://fourhourworkweek.com/2013/07/31/why-and-how-creative-people-need-to-say-no/.

Sills, Judith. "The Power of No." *Psychology Today*, November 5, 2013. https://www.psychologytoday.com/articles/201311/the-power-no.

Patrick, Vanessa M., and Henrik Hagtvedt. "'I Don't' versus I Can't': When Empowered Refusal Motivates Goal-Directed Behavior.' *Journal of Consumer Research* 39, no. 2 (August 2012), 371-381. doi:10.1086/663212.

## CHAPTER 10

Beutel, Manfred E., Eva M. Klein, Stefan Aufenanger, Elmar Brähler, Michael Dreier, Kai W. Müller, Oliver Quiring, et al. "Procrastination, Distress and Life Satisfaction across the Age Range – A German Representative Community Study." *PLOS ONE* 11, no. 2 (February 2016), e0148054. doi:10.1371/journal.pone.0148054.

Blouin-Hudon, Eve-Marie C., and Timothy A. Pychyl. "Experiencing the temporally extended self: Initial support for the role of affective states, vivid mental imagery, and future self-continuity in the prediction of academic procrastination." *Personality and Individual Differences* 86 (November 2015), 50-56. doi:10.1016/j.paid.2015.06.003.

Ersner-Hershfield, Hal, M. T. Garton, Kacey Ballard, Gregory R. Samanez-Larkin, and Brian Knutson. "Don't stop thinking about tomorrow: Individual differences in future self-continuity account for saving." *Judgment and Decision Making* 4, no. 4 (June 2009), 280-286. journal.sjdm.org/9310/jdm9310.pdf.

*Happy Feet*. Directed by George Miller, Warren Coleman, and Judy Morris. 2006. Burbank, CA: Warner Bros., 2007. Film. Happy Feet: (Check out the clip here: https://www.youtube.com/watch?v=kADoPHlV02s)

Sirois, Fuschia, and Timothy Pychyl. "Procrastination and the Priority of Short-Term Mood Regulation: Consequences for Future Self." *Social and Personality Psychology Compass* 7, no. 2 (2013), 115-127. doi:10.1111/spc3.12011.

## CHAPTER 11

Brindle, Ryan C., and Sarah M. Conklin. "Daytime Sleep Accelerates Cardiovascular Recovery after Psychological Stress." *International Journal of Behavioral Medicine* 19, no. 1 (2011), 111-114. doi:10.1007/s12529-011-9150-0.

Cai, D. J., S. A. Mednick, E. M. Harrison, J. C. Kanady, and S. C. Mednick. "REM, not incubation, improves creativity by priming associative networks." *Proceedings of the National Academy of Sciences* 106, no. 25 (January 2009), 10130-10134. doi:10.1073/pnas.0900271106.

De Bloom, Jessica, Simone Ritter, Jana Kühnel, Jennifer Reinders, and Sabine Geurts. "Vacation from work: A 'ticket to creativity'?" *Tourism Management* 44 (October 2014), 164-171. doi:10.1016/j.tourman.2014.03.013.

Dhand, Rajiv, and Harjyot Sohal. "Good sleep, bad sleep! The role of daytime naps in healthy adults." *Current Opinion in Internal Medicine* 6, no. 1 (2007), 91-94. doi:10.1097/01.mcp.0000245703.92311.d0.

Fottrell, Quentin. "Americans take half of their paid vacation, but Chinese take less." *MarketWatch*, September 11, 2015. http://www.marketwatch.com/story/americans-only-take-half-of-their-paid-vacation-2014-04-03.

Hayashi, Mitsuo, Makiko Watanabe, and Tadao Hori. "The effects of a 20 min nap in the mid-afternoon on mood, performance and EEG activity." *Clinical Neurophysiology* 110, no. 2 (February 1999), 272-279. doi:10.1016/s1388-2457(98)00003-0.

Kivimäki, Mika, Markus Jokela, Solja T. Nyberg, Archana Singh-Manoux, Eleonor I. Fransson, Lars Alfredsson, Jakob B. Bjorner, et al. "Long working hours and risk of coronary heart disease and stroke: a systematic review and meta-analysis of published and unpublished data for 603 838 individuals." *The Lancet* 386, no. 10005 (October 2015), 1739–1746. http://www.thelancet.com/journals/lancet/article/PIIS0140-6736%2815%2960295-1/abstract.

Mednick, Sara C., Denise J. Cai, Jennifer Kanady, and Sean P. Drummond. "Comparing the benefits of caffeine, naps and placebo on verbal, motor and perceptual memory." *Behavioural Brain Research* 193, no. 1 (November 2008), 79-86. doi:10.1016/j.bbr.2008.04.028.

"Napping Benefits & Tips - National Sleep Foundation." National Sleep Foundation - Sleep Research & Education. Accessed January 5, 2017. https://sleepfoundation.org/sleep-topics/napping.

"Napping May Not Be Such a No-no." *Harvard Health Letter*. November 2009 http://www.health.harvard.edu/newsletter_article/napping-may-not-be-such-a-no-no.

Naska, Androniki. "Siesta in Healthy Adults and Coronary Mortality in the General Population." *Archives of Internal Medicine* 167, no. 3 (February 2007), 296. doi:10.1001/archinte.167.3.296.

"Overwhelmed America Infographic." Project: Time Off. Accessed January 5, 2017. http://www.projecttimeoff.com/resources/infographics/overwhelmed-america-infographic.

Paddock, Catharine. "Napping Boosts Brain Power." *Medical News Today*, February 24, 2010. http://www.medicalnewstoday.com/articles/180304.php.

Reid, Erin. "Embracing, Passing, Revealing, and the Ideal Worker Image: How People Navigate Expected and Experienced Professional Identities." *Organization Science* 26, no. 4 (April 2015), 997-1017. doi:10.1287/orsc.2015.0975.

Rosekind, Mark R., Roy M. Smith, Donna L. Miller, Elizabeth L. Co, Kevin B. Gregory, Lissa L. Webbon, Philippa H. Gander, and J. V. Lebacqz. "Alertness management: strategic naps in operational settings." *Journal of Sleep Research* 4 (1995), 62-66. doi:10.1111/j.1365-2869.1995.tb00229.x.

Smith-Coggins, Rebecca, Steven K. Howard, Dat T. Mac, Cynthia Wang, Sharon Kwan, Mark R. Rosekind, Yasser Sowb, Raymond Balise, Joel Levis, and David M. Gaba. "Improving Alertness and Performance in Emergency Department Physicians and Nurses: The Use of Planned Naps." *Annals of Emergency Medicine* 48, no. 5 (November 2006), 596-604.e3. doi:10.1016/j.annemergmed.2006.02.005.

Turner, Maria S. "Frontier: REM Sleep Stimulates Creativity." Dana Foundation - Home. Last modified June 2009. http://dana.org/Publications/Brainwork/Details.aspx?id=43783.

Virtanen, M., A. Singh-Manoux, J. E. Ferrie, D. Gimeno, M. G. Marmot, M. Elovainio, M. Jokela, J. Vahtera, and M. Kivimaki. "Long Working Hours and Cognitive Function: The Whitehall II Study." *American Journal of Epidemiology* 169, no. 5 (2008), 596-605. doi:10.1093/aje/kwn382.

## CHAPTER 12

Cappelli, Peter, and Steve Inskeep. "Study: Young Employees Waste Time at Work : NPR." NPR.org. Last modified August 1, 2007. http://www.npr.org/templates/story/story.php?storyId=12418102.

## CHAPTER 13

Alhola, Paula, and Päivi Polo-Kantola. "Sleep deprivation: Impact on cognitive performance." *Neuropsychiatr Dis Treat* 3, no. 5 (October 2007), 553–567. https://www.ncbi.nlm.nih.gov/pmc/articles/PMC2656292/.

Amabile, T. M., C. N. Hadley, and S. J. Kramer. "Creativity under the gun." *Harvard Business Review* 80, no. 8 (2002), 52-61. http://europepmc.org/abstract/MED/12195920/reload=0;jsessionid=fObN5ldi38y4x7wKcTqQ.18.

Angier, Natalie. "Brain Is a Co-Conspirator in a Vicious Stress Loop." *The New York Times* (New York), August 17, 2009. http://www.nytimes.com/2009/08/18/science/18angier.html?_r=3&em.

Blanchette, David, Stephen Ramocki, John O'del, and Michael Casey. "Aerobic Exercise and Creative Potential: Immediate and Residual Effects." *Creativity Research Journal* 17, no. 2 (2005), 257-264. doi:10.1207/s15326934crj1702&3_10.

Caldwell, Emily. "Stress Interferes With Problem-Solving; Beta-Blocker May Help." Ohio State Research and Innovation Communications. Last modified November 16, 2005. https://researchnews.osu.edu/archive/strsbeta.htm.

Card, Orson Scott. *How to Write Science Fiction & Fantasy*. Cincinnati, Ohio: Writer's Digest Books, 2001.

Dias-Ferreira, E., J. C. Sousa, I. Melo, P. Morgado, A. R. Mesquita, J. J. Cerqueira, R. M. Costa, and N. Sousa. "Chronic Stress Causes Frontostriatal Reorganization and Affects Decision-Making." *Science* 325, no. 5940 (July 2009), 621-625. doi:10.1126/science.1171203.

Eastman, Quinn. "High-fructose Diet in Adolescence May Exacerbate Depressive-like Behavior | Emory University | Atlanta, GA." Emory News Center | Emory University | Atlanta GA. Last modified November 19, 2014. http://www.news.emory.edu/stories/2014/11/fructose_adolescents_sfn/index.html.

"Exercise Fuels the Brain's Stress Busters." American Psychological Association. Accessed January 3, 2017. http://www.apa.org/helpcenter/exercise-stress.aspx.

Fahmy, Sam. "Low-intensity Exercise Reduces Fatigue Symptoms by 65 Percent, Study Finds | UGA Today." UGA Today | News Releases. Last modified February 28 2008. http://news.uga.edu/releases/article/low-intensity-exercise-reduces-fatigue-symptoms-by-65-percent-study-finds/.

Hemingway, Ernest. *A Movable Feast*. New York: Scribner, 1964.

Hryhorczuk, Cecile, Marc Florea, Demetra Rodaros, Isabelle Poirier, Caroline Daneault, Christine Des Rosiers, Andreas Arvanitogiannis, Thierry Alquier, and Stephanie Fulton. "Dampened Mesolimbic Dopamine Function and Signaling by Saturated but not Monounsaturated Dietary Lipids." *Neuropsychopharmacology* 41, no. 3 (2015), 811-821. doi:10.1038/npp.2015.207.

Kelly, Morgan. "Princeton University - Exercise Reorganizes the Brain to Be

More Resilient to Stress." Princeton University - Home. Last modified July 3, 2013. https://www.princeton.edu/main/news/archive/S37/28/70Q72/index.xml?section=topstories.

Killgore, William D. "Effects of sleep deprivation on cognition." *Progress in Brain Research*, no. 185 (2010), 105-129. doi:10.1016/b978-0-444-53702-7.00007-5.

Magnusson, K.R., L. Hauck, B.M. Jeffrey, V. Elias, A. Humphrey, R. Nath, A. Perrone, and L.E. Bermudez. "Relationships between diet-related changes in the gut microbiome and cognitive flexibility." *Neuroscience* 300 (August 2015), 128-140. doi:10.1016/j.neuroscience.2015.05.016.

Martin, Judy. "Employee Brain on Stress Can Quash Creativity And Competitive Edge." *Forbes*, September 5, 2012. http://www.forbes.com/sites/work-in-progress/2012/09/05/employee-brain-on-stress-can-quash-creativity-competitive-edge/#6a43c8e61500.

Puetz, Timothy W., Patrick J. O'Connor, and Rod K. Dishman. "Effects of chronic exercise on feelings of energy and fatigue: A quantitative synthesis." *Psychological Bulletin* 132, no. 6 (2006), 866-876. doi:10.1037/0033-2909.132.6.866.

Rodriguez, Tori. "Creativity Predicts a Longer Life." *Scientific American Mind*, September 1, 2012. http://www.scientificamerican.com/article/open-mind-longer-life/.

S. Colzato, Lorenza, Ayca Szapora, Justine N. Pannekoek, and Bernhard Hommel. "The impact of physical exercise on convergent and divergent thinking." *Frontiers in Human Neuroscience* 7 (December 2013). doi:10.3389/fnhum.2013.00824.

Schaefer, Sabine, Martin Lövdén, Birgit Wieckhorst, and Ulman Lindenberger. "Cognitive performance is improved while walking: Differences in cognitive–sensorimotor couplings between children and young adults." *European Journal of Developmental Psychology* 7, no. 3 (2010), 371-389. doi:10.1080/17405620802535666.

Schmidt, Elaine. "This is Your Brain on Sugar: UCLA Study Shows High-fructose Diet Sabotages Learning, Memory | UCLA." UCLA Newsroom. Last modified May 15, 2012. http://newsroom.ucla.edu/releases/this-is-your-brain-on-sugar-ucla-233992.

Sánchez-Villegas, Almudena, Patricia Henríquez-Sánchez, Miguel Ruiz-Canela, Francisca Lahortiga, Patricio Molero, Estefanía Toledo, and Miguel A. Martínez-González. "A longitudinal analysis of diet quality scores and the risk of incident depression in the SUN Project." *BMC Medicine* 13, no. 1 (September 2015). doi:10.1186/s12916-015-0428-y.

Talbot, Reg, Cary Cooper, and Steve Barrow. "Creativity and Stress." *Creativity and Innovation Management* 1, no. 4 (December 1992), 183-193. doi:10.1111/j.1467-8691.1992.tb00052.x.

Tillisch, Kirsten, Jennifer Labus, Lisa Kilpatrick, Zhiguo Jiang, Jean Stains, Bahar Ebrat, Denis Guyonnet, et al. "Consumption of Fermented Milk Product With Probiotic Modulates Brain Activity." *Gastroenterology* 144, no 7 (June 2013), 1394-1401.e4. doi:10.1053/j.gastro.2013.02.043.

Von Thiele Schwarz, Ulrica, and Henna Hasson. "Employee Self-rated Productivity and Objective Organizational Production Levels." *Journal of Occupational and Environmental Medicine* 53, no. 8 (2011), 838-844. doi:10.1097/jom.0b013e31822589c2.

Voss, Michael W. "Plasticity of brain networks in a randomized intervention trial of exercise training in older adults." *Frontiers in Aging Neuroscience* 2, no. 32 (August 2010). doi:10.3389/fnagi.2010.00032.

Wieth, Mareike B., and Rose T. Zacks. "Time of day effects on problem solving: When the non-optimal is optimal." *Thinking & Reasoning* 17, no. 4 (2011), 387-401. doi:10.1080/13546783.2011.625663.

## CHAPTER 14

Pressfield, Steven. "Panic Attacks." Steven Pressfield. Last modified May 2, 2014. http://www.stevenpressfield.com/2014/05/panic-attacks/.

Stern, Abby. "Cameron Diaz Was Scared Before the Release of 1st Book." *People*, November 6, 2016. http://people.com/books/cameron-diaz-was-scared-and-debilitated-before-the-release-of-her-first-book/.

Warrell, Margie. "Afraid Of Being 'Found Out?' How To Overcome Impostor Syndrome." *Forbes*, April 3, 2014. http://www.forbes.com/sites/margiewarrell/2014/04/03/impostor-syndrome/#333aaba0eb9d.

## CHAPTER 15

Borchard, Therese J. "Good Perfectionism Versus Bad Perfectionism." World of

Psychology. Last modified May 16, 2011. http://psychcentral.com/blog/archives/2011/05/16/good-perfectionism-versus-bad-perfectionism/.

Dahl, Melissa. "How Much Can You Really Change After You Turn 30?" *Science of Us*, November 24, 2014. http://nymag.com/scienceofus/2014/11/how-much-can-you-really-change-after-30.html.

Goleman, Daniel. "Personality—Major Traits Found Stable Through Life." *The New York Times*, June 9, 1987. http://www.nytimes.com/1987/06/09/science/personality-major-traits-found-stable-through-life.html?pagewanted=all.

MacDonald, Ann. "How to Become a Better Perfectionist." *Harvard Health Blog*, September 12, 2011. http://www.health.harvard.edu/blog/how-to-become-a-better-perfectionist-201109123326.

## CHAPTER 16

Bielski, Zosia. "We Wish You a Frantic Christmas: Festive Letters Shed Light on Holidays." *The Globe and Mail*, December 4, 2014. http://www.theglobeandmail.com/life/holiday-guide/holiday-survival-guide/we-wish-you-a-frantic-christmas-festive-letters-shed-light-on-holidays/article21954677/.

"'Dear Friends and Family:' What Does Your Annual Holiday Letter Say About You? - Research and Creative Activity (NDSU)." NDSU - North Dakota State University. Last modified December 14, 2010. https://www.ndsu.edu/research/newsroom/feature_stories2010/dear_friends_and_family_what_does_your_annual_holiday_letter_say_about_you/.

Immordino-Yang, M. H., J. A. Christodoulou, and V. Singh. "Rest Is Not Idleness: Implications of the Brain's Default Mode for Human Development and Education." *Perspectives on Psychological Science* 7, no. 4 (July 2012), 352-364. doi:10.1177/1745691612447308.

Kajitani, Shinya, Colin McKenzie, and Kei Sakata. *Use It Too Much and Lose It? The Effect of Working Hours on Cognitive Ability*. Victoria, Australia: Melbourne Institute Working Paper No. 7/16, 2016. https://www.melbourneinstitute.com/downloads/working_paper_series/wp2016n07.pdf.

Marriner, Cosima. "Why You Shouldn't Work More Than 25 Hours a Week." *The Sydney Morning Herald* (Sydney), April 17, 2016. http:// http://www.

smh.com.au/national/why-you-shouldnt-work-more-than-25-hours-a-week-20160415-go7ert.html.

O'Brien, Kiera, and Sarah Shaffi. "Tyler is Top-selling Man Booker Longlisted Title." *The Bookseller*, September 10, 2015. http://www.thebookseller.com/news/anne-tyler-top-selling-man-booker-longlisted-title-312012.

Parrish, Shane. "In Praise of Idleness: The Productivity Secret Nobody Talks About." *Observer*, May 15, 2014. http://observer.com/2014/05/in-praise-of-idleness-the-productivity-secret-nobody-talks-about/.

Pencavel, John. *The Productivity of Working Hours*. Bonn, Germany: Discussion Paper Series, Forschungsinstitut zur Zukunft der Arbeit Institute for the Study of Labor, 2014. http://ftp.iza.org/dp8129.pdf.

Saad, Lydia. "The "40-Hour" Workweek Is Actually Longer — by Seven Hours | Gallup." Gallup.com. Last modified August 29, 2014. http://www.gallup.com/poll/175286/hour-workweek-actually-longer-seven-hours.aspx.

Schulte, Brigid. "Why Being Too Busy Makes Us Feel So Good." *The Washington Post* (Washington, D.C.), March 14, 2014. https://www.washingtonpost.com/opinions/why-being-too-busy-makes-us-feel-so-good/2014/03/14/c098f6c8-9e81-11e3-a050-dc3322a94fa7_story.html?utm_term=.df1574985cf0.

Sullivan, Bob. "Working More Than 50 Hours Makes You Less Productive." *CNBC*, January 26, 2015. http://www.cnbc.com/2015/01/26/working-more-than-50-hours-makes-you-less-productive.html.

Ursrey, Lawton. "Your Brain Unplugged: Proof That Spacing Out Makes You More Effective." *Forbes*, May 16, 2014. http://www.forbes.com/sites/lawtonursrey/2014/05/16/your-brain-unplugged-proof-that-spacing-out-makes-you-more-effective/#191c1396e20e.

*The Wages of Writing*. New York, NY: The Authors Guild, 2015. https://docs.google.com/viewerng/viewer?url=https://www.authorsguild.org/wp-content/uploads/2015/09/WagesofWriting_Final_10-22-15.pdf&hl=en.

## CHAPTER 17

No references.

## CHAPTER 18

Boaler, Jo, and Carol Dweck. *Mathematical Mindsets: Unleashing Students' Poten-

*tial Through Creative Math, Inspiring Messages, and Innovative Teaching*. San Francisco: Jossey-Bass, 2016.

Chandler, Michael A. "In schools, self-esteem boosting is losing favor to rigor, finer-tuned praise." *The Washington Post* (Washington, D.C.), January 15, 2012. https://www.washingtonpost.com/local/education/in-schools-self-esteem-boosting-is-losing-favor-to-rigor-finer-tuned-praise/2012/01/11/gIQAXFnF1P_story.html?utm_term=.4720c20dd443.

Kohn, Alfie. "The Truth About Self-Esteem." Alfie Kohn. Last modified December 1994. www.alfiekohn.org/article/truth-self-esteem/.

Loveless, Tom. "The 2006 Brown Center Report on American Education: How Well Are American Students Learning? Institution." Brookings. Last modified October 1, 2006. https://www.brookings.edu/research/the-2006-brown-center-report-on-american-education-how-well-are-american-students-learning/.

Marsh, Herbert W., and Andrew J. Martin. "Academic self-concept and academic achievement: Relations and causal ordering." *British Journal of Educational Psychology* 81, no. 1 (March 2011), 59-77. doi:10.1348/000709910x503501.

Pottebaum, Sheila M., Timothy Z. Keith, and Stewart W. Ehly. "Is There a Causal Relation between Self-Concept and Academic Achievement?" *The Journal of Educational Research* 79, no. 3 (January/February 1986), 140-144. doi:10.1080/00220671.1986.10885665.

Wood, Joanne V., W.Q. Elaine Perunovic, and John W. Lee. "Positive Self-Statements: Power for Some, Peril for Others." *Psychological Science* 20, no. 7 (July 2009), 860-866. doi:10.1111/j.1467-9280.2009.02370.x.

## CHAPTER 19

Butler, Timothy. *Getting Unstuck: A Guide to Discovering Your Next Career Path*. Boston, Mass: Harvard Business Press, 2010.

**NOTE:** Butler gives credit to American psychologist Henry Murray and psychologist David McClelland for their work in researching and identifying the three needs.

## CHAPTER 20

No references.

## CHAPTER 21
No references.

## CHAPTER 22
Duckworth, Angela L., and Lauren Eskreis-Winkler. "True Grit." *The Observer*, April 2013. http://www.psychologicalscience.org/observer/true-grit#.WGsxnvMzwy4.

Duckworth, Angela L., Christopher Peterson, Michael D. Matthews, and Dennis R. Kelly. "Grit: Perseverance and passion for long-term goals." *Journal of Personality and Social Psychology* 92, no. 6 (2007), 1087-1101. doi:10.1037/0022-3514.92.6.1087.

Willingham, Warren W. *Success in College: The Role of Personal Qualities and Academic Ability*. New York: College Entrance Examination Board, 1985.

## CHAPTER 23
Gazica, Michele W., and Paul E. Spector. "A comparison of individuals with unanswered callings to those with no calling at all." *Journal of Vocational Behavior* 91 (December 2015), 1-10. doi:10.1016/j.jvb.2015.08.008.

# ACKNOWLEDGMENTS

I have so many people to thank for their help with this project. First of all I want to thank my family for their enduring support and encouragement. I have the strength and the motivation to go after my dreams because of you.

Next, I want to thank my editor, P. J. Dempsey, not only for her sharp eye on the content and the prose, but her invaluable experience in writing self-help in general. You helped me write with more confidence and for that I'm extremely grateful.

Thank you to editor Anne Cole Norman for a helpful second read-through, and a special thank you to Mary Story for her sharp proofreading eye.

A huge thank you to the extremely talented designers at Damonza book design. You folks are truly amazing in how you brought my vision to life. I will shout your praises to any other writer who's willing to listen!

I'm deeply grateful to Chuck Barrett, a best-selling thriller writer and good friend who was there for me whenever I had yet another question on the whole process of publication. Thanks for your enduring support and for giving so graciously of your time.

Thank you as well to my writer friends (you know who you are) who were willing to give feedback on titles, covers, etc.! You helped guide me to the best choices every time.

Thank you to all Writing and Wellness readers, for your consistent feedback and interest in what I have to share and in this creative life in general.

Finally, I want to express my thanks to all readers of this book. I hope it helps you to feel more joyful and on purpose in your creative life.

## ABOUT THE AUTHOR

**Colleen M. Story** has worked in the creative writing industry for over twenty years. Her novels include *Loreena's Gift*, an Idaho Author Awards first place winner, New Apple Solo Medalist winner, Foreword Reviews' INDIES Book of the Year Awards winner, Reader Views award finalist, and Best Book Awards finalist; and *Rise of the Sidenah*, a North American Book Awards winner and New Apple Book Awards Official Selection.

As a health writer, she's authored thousands of articles for publications like *Healthline* and *Women's Health*; worked with high-profile clients like Gerber Baby Products and Kellogg's; and ghostwritten books on back pain, nutrition, and cancer recovery. She finds most rewarding her work as a motivational speaker and workshop leader, where she helps writers remove mental and emotional blocks and tap into their unique creative powers.

Colleen is the founder of Writing and Wellness (writingandwellness.com), a motivational site helping writers and other creative artists maintain their physical, mental, and emotional health and well-being throughout their careers. Sign up for your free weekly email containing tips for living your best creative life at www.writingandwellness/newsletter.

To find more information on Colleen and her work, please see her website (colleenmstory.com), or follow her on Twitter (@colleen_m_story). She loves to hear from readers—feel free to use the "contact" form on either her website or Writing and Wellness to get in touch with her.

www.ingramcontent.com/pod-product-compliance
Lightning Source LLC
Chambersburg PA
CBHW071158300426
44113CB00009B/1242